THE HEART OF A
CHAMPION

Celebrating the Spirit and Character of Great American Sports Heroes

by Frank Deford

A TEHABI BOOK

TEHABI BOOKS

Tehabi Books developed, designed, and produced *The Heart of a Champion: Celebrating the Spirit and Character of Great American Sports Heroes* and has conceived and produced many award-winning books that are recognized for their strong literary and visual content. Tehabi works with national and international publishers, corporations, institutions, and nonprofit groups to identify, develop, and implement comprehensive publishing programs. Tehabi Books is located in San Diego, California. www.tehabi.com

President and Publisher: Chris Capen
Senior Vice President: Tom Lewis
Vice President of Operations: Sam Lewis
Editorial Director: Nancy Cash
Sales Director: Eric Pinkham
Director, Corporate Publishing: Tim Connolly
Director, Trade Relations: Marty Remmell
Art Director: Curt Boyer
Editor: Terry Spohn
Copy Editor: Marianna Lee
Editorial Assistant: Christine Huynh
Art Director: Curt Boyer
Proofreader: Robin Witkin

Tehabi Books gives its heart-felt thanks for a tremendous team effort in helping to produce this book to Jerry Coleman, Courtney Caress, Jeff Idelson, Chuck Menke, Don Motley, Dan Pinkham, Daniel Siegel, Andy Strasberg, and the great Wheaties Brand and Licensing teams, including Brian Immel, D.J. Christensen, and from the General Mills Archivist Katie Dishman.

Library of Congress Cataloging-in-Publication Data

Deford, Frank.
    The heart of a champion : celebrating the spirit and character of great American sports heroes/ Frank Deford.
        p. cm.
    ISBN 1–55971–837–4 (harcover)
    1. Athletes—United States—Biography. 2. Athletes—United States—Marketing. I Title.

GV697.A1 D394 2002
796'.092'2—dc21
[B]   2002075270

The paper used in this publication meets the minimum requirements of the American National Standard for Information Sciences—Permanence of Paper for Printed Library Materials, ANSI Z39. 48-1992.

First Edition
Printed through Dai Nippon Printing Co., Ltd. in Korea.
10 9 8 7 6 5 4 3 2 1

NORTHWORD

NorthWord Press is an imprint of Creative Publishing international (CPi). Since 1989, NorthWord has published top-quality books on nature, wildlife, and outdoor adventure. NorthWord publishes many of America's finest nature photographers and illustrators, and has a growing line of children's fiction and educational books.

NorthWord Press
Creative Publishing international
President/CEO: Michael Eleftheriou
Vice President/Publisher: Linda Ball
Vice President/Retail Sales & Marketing: Kevin Haas
Executive Editor: Bryan Trandem
Editorial Director: Barbara Harold

Acknowledgments

Wheaties Box Images

Appreciation to General Mills, Inc.

Muhammad Ali, p. 81: Permission of Neil Leifer

Arthur Ashe, p. 163: TM/©2002 The Jeannie Ashe Foundation by CMG Worldwide Inc., www.CMGWorldwide.com

James "Cool Papa" Bell, p. 139: Permission of Connie Brooks

Roy Campanella, p. 159: TM/©2002 Roy Campanella by CMG Worldwide Inc., www.CMGWorldwide.com

Donna de Varona, p. 84: Permission of Donna de Varona

Dale Earnhardt, p. 34: Permission of Sam Bass, Sam Bass Gallery

Chris Evert, p. 62: Permission of Evert Enterprises, Inc.

Bob Feller, p. 160: TM/©2002 Bob Feller by CMG Worldwide Inc., www.CMGWorldwide.com

Jimmie Foxx, p. 154: TM/©2002 Jimmie Foxx by CMG Worldwide Inc., www.CMGWorldwide.com

Lou Gehrig, p. 89: TM/©2002 Lou Gehrig, LLC by CMG Worldwide Inc., www.CMGWorldwide.com

Josh Gibson, p. 139: ©2002 Josh Gibson under exclusive license authorized by Schulte Sports Marketing, Inc. www.schultesprrtsmarketing.com

Henry Greenberg, p. 92: Permission of Stephen D. Greenberg, The Henry Greenberg Trust

Bruce Jenner, p. 9: Permission of Bruce Jenner

Mark McGwire, p. 167: Permission of Hill and Knowlton, Inc., and Tom DiPace Photography

Billy Mills, p. 142: Permission of Billy Mills

Negro Leagues, 75th Anniversary, p. 139: permission of Negro Leagues Baseball Museum

Satchel Paige, p. 139: TM/©2002 Satchel Paige Enterprises by CMG Worldwide Inc., www.CMGWorldwide.com

Walter Payton, p. 56: Permission of the Walter and Connie Payton Foundation

Richard Petty, p. 164: Permission of the Richard Petty Museum, and Sam Bass, Sam Bass Gallery

Mary Lou Retton, p. 164: Permission of Mary Lou Retton

Jerry Rice, p. 23: Permission of Jerry Rice and SFX Football, and NFL Photo

Bob Richards, p. 144: Permission of Robert Richards

Cal Ripken Jr., p. 14: Permission of Cal Ripken Baseball, and Tom DiPace Photography

Jackie Robinson, p. 46: TM/©2002 Rachel Robinson by CMG Worldwide Inc., www.CMGWorldwide.com, and AP/Wide World Photos

Pete Rose, p. 164: TM/©2002 Pete Rose by CMG Worldwide Inc., www.CMGWorldwide.com

Roger Staubach, 132: Permission of Roger Staubach, and Roger Staubach by LeRoy Neiman

Johnny Unitas, p. 162: TM/©2002 Johnny Unitas by CMG Worldwide Inc., www.CMGWorldwide.com; and Johnny Unitas by LeRoy Neiman

1980 U.S. Olympic Hockey Team, p. 107: Used with permission, and Getty Images

1996 U.S. Women's Olympic Gymnastic Team, p. 121: With permission of Amanda Bordon, Amy Chow, Dominique Dawes, Shannon Miller, Dominique Moceanu, Jaycie Phelps, Kerri Strug, and Getty Images.

Jerry West, p. 112: Permission of Jerry West

Laura Wilkinson, p. 167: Permission of Laura Wilkinson, and AP/Wide World Photos

Tiger Woods, p. 27: Used by Permission of ETW Corp. and Paul Severn/Getty Images

Photo Credits

Al Bello/Getty Images: 109a, 111

Al Fenn/TimePix: 125a, 141a, 142a

© Al Messerschmidt/Joe Robbins Photography: 21b, 28-29, 52, 57b, 99b

Al Tielemans/Sports Illustrated: 18-19, AP/Wide World Photos: 12b, 13, 15a, 15b, 16a, 17, 24, 25b, 26b, 26c, 32b, 40b, 41a, 42, 43b, 47a, 47b, 47c, 48b, 50-51, 53a, 53b, 54-55, 57a, 58, 59a, 59b, 60a, 61, 63a, 65, 68b, 69b, 71b, 73, 76, 77b, 80a, 85, 86, 87b, 88, 90, 91a, 91b, 92a, 98, 100a, 105a, 105b, 106b, 109b, 110a, 110b, 113b, 119b, 120b, 122-123, 124b, 126, 127a, 127b, 128a, 128b, 129, 130-131, 137b, 138b, 140, 141b, 145, 146-147, 149, 152a, 152b, 153a, 153d, 153e, 153f, 154c, 154d, 154e, 155a, 155d, 155e, 156c, 156e, 157b, 157d, 157e, 157f, 158d, 158e, 158h, 159c, 159d, 160b, 160d, 160e, 161c, 161d, 162b, 162c, 162d, 162e, 163a, 163d, 163e, 163g, 164a, 164c, 164d, 164e, 164f, 165e, 165g, 166d, 166e, 166f, 167b, 167c, 167d, 167e, 167f, 168a

Art Rickerby/TimePix: 84a

Art Shay/TimePix: 148a

© Bettmann/CORBIS: 4-5, 43a, 45, 66-67, 113a, 114-115, 134b

Bob Gomel/TimePix: 82, 83

Bob Martin/Getty Images: 166b

Caryn Levy/Sports Illustrated: 38-39

CIA Stock Photo, Inc.: 35a, 36, 37

Copyright Empics Ltd.: 97b, 100b, 101, 102-103, 119a, 120a, 120c

Dave Sandford/Hockey Hall of Fame: 158f

© David Durochix/Joe Robbins Photography: 20, 22, 23

David Mills/Reuters/TimePix: 35b

Doug Pensinger/Getty Images: 69a

© Duomo/CORBIS: 6-7

© Duomo/Paul J. Sutton: 30, 31a, 31b, 32a, 118

© Duomo/Steven E. Sutton: 96b

Ezra O. Shaw/Getty Images: 99a

Flip Schulke/Black Star/TimePix: 77a

General Mills/photographer: 9, 27, 56, 60b, 62, 72, 84b, 89, 92b, 112, 142b, 152c, 153b, 154a, 154f, 155h, 156b, 156f, 157g, 157j, 158g, 159f, 160a, 161f, 161g, 162f, 163b, 163f, 164b, 164g, 164h, 165f, 166g, 167g

George Long/Sports Illustrated: 97a

George Silk/TimePix: 136

George Strock/TimePix: 138a

Heinz Kluetmeier/Sports Illustrated: 33, 104, 106a

Herb Scharfman/TimePix: 78-79, 133a, 133b

Herbert Gehr/TimePix: 157h

Hy Peskin/TimePix: 158c

IOC/Olympic Museum Collection: 158a

J.R. Eyerman/TimePix: 158b

James Drake/ Sports Illustrated: 135 set # X16132

Jason Cohn/Reuters/TimePix: 70

Jerry Lodriguss/TimePix: 21a

Jim Ruymen/Reuters/TimePix: 25a

Joe Robbins Photography: 23, 26a

Loomis Dean/TimePix: 49

Manny Millan/Sports Illustrated: 63b

Mike Blake/Reuters/TimePix: 74-75

Mike Powell/Getty Images: 165c, 165d

Mike Segar/Reuters/TimePix: 12c

Peter Read Miller/Sports Illustrated: 117a

Pix Inc/TimePix: 156d

Private Collection: 148b

Ralph Crane/TimePix: 125b

Kimimasa Mayama /Reuters /TimePix: 10-11

Reuters/TimePix: 168c

Rick Stewart/Getty Images: 166c, 167a

Ronald C. Modra/Sports Illustrated: 94-95 X51638, 108 X51638

Ronald C. Modra/TimePix: 165b

© Scott Boehm/Joe Robbins Photography: 71a

Shaun Best/Reuters/TimePix: 168b

Sheedy & Long/Sports Illustrated: 116b

Steve Powell/Getty Images: 64b

Ted Polumbaum/TimePix: 41b, 160c

The San Diego Hall of Champions: 143

Time Magazine, © Time Inc./TimePix: 80c, 160f, 162g

Tony Triolo/TimePix: 163c

Transcendental Graphics: 2-3, 16b, 44a, 48a, 60c, 80b, 87a, 93, 117b, 137a, 142c, 150-151, 153c, 153g, 153h, 154b, 154g, 155b, 155c, 155f, 155g, 156a 157a, 157c, 157i, 158b, 159a, 159e, 159g, 160g, 161a, 161e, 161h, 162a, 162h, 165a, 166a

© Underwood & Underwood/CORBIS: 44b

Walter Iooss, Jr./Sports Illustrated: 64a, 116a, 134a

Contents

"To believe in the heroic makes heroes." —BENJAMIN DISRAELI

INTRODUCTION

IN A NATION as large and diverse as the United States, even with more sophisticated communication systems than many ever envisioned possible, we have become ever more fragmented. We find ourselves needing to share some common icons and images, and even if athletes may be insignificant in the full scheme of things, they serve some real national function in joining us together.

I don't know if we really, consciously, view athletes as heroes. But doing something difficult with proficiency and grace under pressure with millions of people watching is certainly admirable—and, yes, heroic in the spectacular, if not the noble, sense.

Anyway, athletes have become our surrogate heroes, and that's fair enough. We used to look first to our warriors, men sitting high in the saddle facing down musket fire, as our *beau ideals*. Television has made war too close and palpable, though, to glamorize it in any way. Besides, a battlefield of smart bombs has become too technological to conjure up an individual like Sergeant York—let alone a Washington or Jackson or MacArthur. Moreover, in a computerized world, men and women who perform old-fashioned physical feats of wonder appear even more attractive. Who doesn't dream about hitting a home run or throwing a touchdown pass on third and long? "By a man's heroes, ye shall know him," Robert Penn Warren said. So, too, by a man's—and a woman's—fantasies.

Athletes are called role models, but they're not. They're dream models. We imagine ourselves in their places in our daydreams. It has been so since we were children witnessing their triumphs over breakfast on the back of a Wheaties box and feeling our own possibilities expand. We look up to the great athlete because a sports star is so visible and so beguiling, but also, so classical. Athletes not only join us together in this more complicated culture, they connect us to the simpler past. In their glory, they make us feel more whole. ★

General Mills

WHEATIES ®

WHOLE WHEAT FLAKES

"Breakfast of Champions".

FORTIFIED TO **25%** OF DAILY NEEDS FOR 7 VITAMINS & IRON ESTABLISHED BY U.S. GOVERNMENT

BRUCE JENNER
*Olympic
Decathlon Champion*

WHEATIES SPORTS FEDERATION
Presents
"Be A Sport"
SEE BACK PANEL

**A GOOD SOURCE OF
NATURAL BRAN FIBER**

K

NET WT 8 OZ (226 grams)

COMMITMENT

"The moment one definitely commits oneself,
then providence moves too." —JOHANN WOLFGANG VON GOETHE

COMMITMENT

NO ONE DISPUTES that the modern athlete is a finer physical specimen than players of times past. The competitor today is larger, faster, stronger. Men and women who excel at sports now must also devote more time to their discipline. Likewise are they better rewarded. That seems fair enough. After all, actors and businessmen and clergy (and writers) are also paid better nowadays. But this prosperity sometimes leads to the new wives' tale that these athletes are not so devoted to their sport as the old heroes, who, we are assured, played for the sheer love of the game.

Cal Ripken Jr. homers at the 2001 All-Star game.

This attitude is heightened by the feeling that these sweaty mercenaries lack the loyalty of their forebears. It is certainly true that few modern stars play out their careers with one team. Tony Gwynn, Kirby Puckett, Dan Marino, and Larry Bird may be of a dying breed, but for wearing one uniform all their pro life long, are they really any finer, any more dedicated, than, say, Dave Winfield, Roger Clemens, Wayne Gretzky, and Clyde Drexler? No, the ground has shifted, and, with that shift it has become easier and more likely for the best players to change allegiance. Does that make them any flightier, any less committed to excellence?

Jerry Rice catches a pass in the playoffs, January 19, 2002

It is also true, if not so often commented on, that today the best players in most sports tend to stay in the game longer. Should this, in turn, reflect badly on the old-timers? Not really. Didn't they love their sport enough to stay with it? Sure they did. It is just that the players of the past were often not financially able to remain in sports. Nor could they work enough to stay in good shape; they needed to take off-season jobs. They needed to give up childish things.

One of my favorite sport reflections is inscribed on a plaque that faces you as you enter the Palestra, that grand old arena in Philadelphia. It reads:

To play the game is great

To win the game is greater

To love the game is the greatest of all

And, therefore it is to sport, rather than to any particular franchise, that athletes must first pay fealty.

It is easy, of course, to devote yourself to an enterprise you are good at. Easier still to submit to something you love. "Work is more fun than fun," Noel Coward said. Easiest of all to dedicate yourself to something you are highly paid for. So perhaps we should pay less attention to the famous, best athletes. Perhaps Jim Bouton's story best exemplifies pure commitment to sport.

As a boy Bouton was a skinny little thing, more fan than prospect. But suddenly he had an Arm. The best pitchers' arms are, in fact, almost a thing apart rather than an actual appendage to the body. How else can normal-sized people like Nolan Ryan or Pedro Martinez throw a ball so fast? With his arm, Bouton became a star pitcher, a bona fide World Series hero. Then his arm deserted him, and he was out of the game at an early age (and a pariah, too, since he had written the allegedly sacrilegious memoir, *Ball Four*).

Bouton became a successful television announcer, but he kept playing baseball on the side, as other onetime players might take up golf. He developed the knuckleball, a funky pitch that puts little strain on the arm, and after six years away, he decided to try a comeback. That meant giving up a lucrative job, taking out a second mortgage, and leaving his family. But damn if Bouton didn't make it back to the majors at the age of thirty-nine, win a game, save another, and earn a contract offer for the next year.

Bruce Jenner, 1976 Olympic decathlon champion

So what did Bouton do then? He turned the offer down. The challenge, he discovered, had been in committing himself to trying to overcome all odds and get back into the game. Once he had achieved that, the satisfaction was greater than any subsequent success he might enjoy. He walked away from the majors and returned to the weekend semipro games. To love the game is the greatest of all.

The athletes we admire most may have, like Bouton, good arms or good legs or muscle or, even, as we say, a good head on their shoulders. But it is the heart and guts we celebrate most. Those are the best qualities of an athlete, for however superior, physically, human beings may have become, there is no evidence that we ever improve intrinsically. There always have been and always will be a few athletes with more drive and devotion than their colleagues. That commitment doesn't ensure victory, of course, but it sustains sport and brings it closest to honor and purity. ★

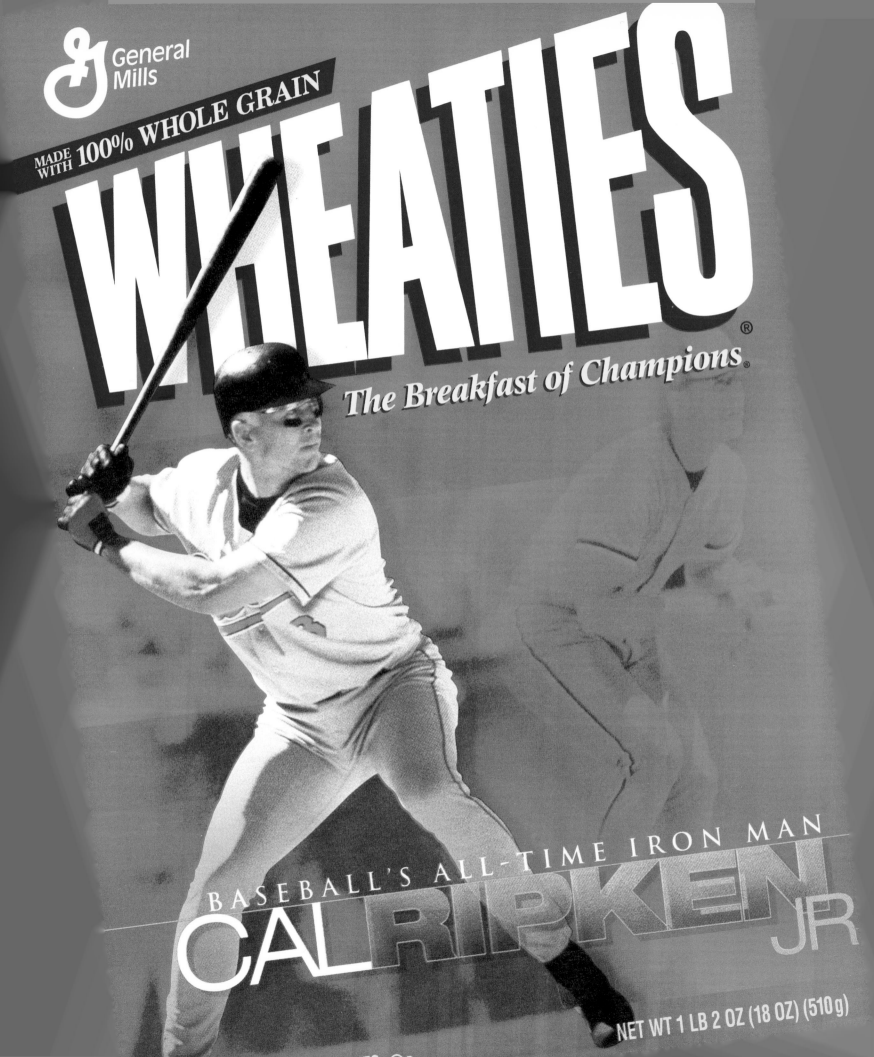

WHEREAS MICHAEL JORDAN was indisputably the greatest athlete in the last part of the twentieth century, Cal Ripken Jr. was just as distinctive, even symbolic. He was, simply, The Athlete. In playing 2,632 consecutive games from 1982 to 1999, Ripken achieved an odd sort of heroic stature. On the one hand he was superman and on the other he was everyman.

Cal Ripkin Jr., Fenway Park, Boston, June 10, 1983

In the same contradictory fashion, Ripken was of two minds himself about the streak. First, it rather annoyed him that it overshadowed almost everything else that he did. He was, after all, a player who was an MVP, an All-Star MVP, who would amass more than three thousand hits and four hundred home runs, who would set fielding records for shortstops. Indeed, at 6-feet-4, 220 pounds, Ripken redefined the physical model of the ideal shortstop; he changed the game—hardly a guy who simply showed up every day with his lunch bucket.

Yet those who knew him well were also aware that nothing could get his back up

IRON MAN
CAL RIPKEN JR.

more than some well-meaning friend suggesting he should maybe sit and rest for a day or two like other mortals. The only one who ever successfully did that was his father, Cal Sr., who, as the Orioles manager, pulled his son out of a lopsided game in 1987, thereby ending a record streak of 8,243 consecutive innings that Junior had played in, out after every out. Enough was enough.

Lou Gehrig, the Iron Horse of lore, had set the record of 2,130 straight games. It was the one record that could surely never be approached, let alone exceeded. But then, strange as it is to say, Ripken managed to pass it rather effortlessly. Only a sprained ankle in 1985 and a twisted right knee in 1993 even mildly threatened to keep him off the field for a day. It all seemed rather amazing. Gertrude Stein made Oakland famous saying, "There's no *there* there." Ripken was the other way round. He was just . . . *there*.

★

Cal Ripken Jr.'s baseball wasn't restricted to inside the lines in his beloved Baltimore. It was played throughout the community, at hospitals and schools, at community gatherings and impromptu autograph sessions after home games that could last as long as the game had.

History away from the ballpark attached more meaning to the man and his achievement, too. To take nothing away from the estimable Gehrig, most of his streak came during the Depression when jobs were hard to come by, so a little extra credit accrued to honest labor. Ripken, on the other hand, was Man at Work at a time when the livin' was easy and ballplayers in particular had taken on the image of spoiled brats.

Billy Ripken, Cal Ripken Sr., and Cal Ripken Jr., left to right, in 1987

Instilled in Ripken, however, were all the old-fashioned American values. He was not taught merely to practice, for example; his father had instructed him in "perfect practice." To watch Ripken take batting practice was to see him first bunt, then try to slap balls to the right to work on moving up the runner. It even made him all the more down-home that he played not only for his father—Cal Sr. was his first Oriole coach, then his manager—but alongside his younger brother, Billy, who toiled at second base for several seasons as Cal's double-play partner.

Neither did Ripken need the streak to prove his steadfastness. After all, he dressed the part every day, spending his whole career in the Oriole system. There was even something appropriate about his address. Baltimore is the quintessential old workingman's town, and so the qualities that Ripken upheld best reflected the people he played before. As much as any modern star, he understood, too, what he meant to his fans. Especially as the streak moved toward the record, Ripken would make himself available for autographs, often for an hour or so after a game, not only signing his name but pausing to engage his admirers in treasured conversations.

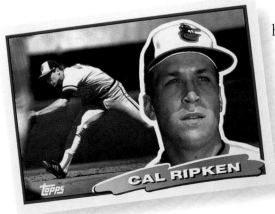
CAL RIPKEN

But more than just being an Oriole, Ripken was a home boy. He came from Havre de Grace, Maryland, near Baltimore, a birthplace of natural symmetry for such a great player. Havre de Grace is fixed at the mouth of the Susquehanna River. If you trace the Susquehanna two hundred miles north, its headwaters flow from a little village named Cooperstown, home of the Baseball Hall of Fame. ★

Cal Ripken's record of consecutive games played, as well as his hitting records, often overshadowed his defensive ability. Indeed, he never tried to protect his body if there was a chance to make a play. He won two Gold Gloves at shortstop as the league's best defensive player at the position, and in 1990 made just three errors in 161 games.

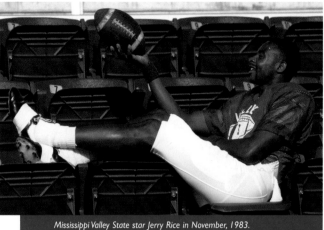

THE LATE GEORGE YOUNG, the sage old general manager of the New York Giants, use to rail at what he called "underwear decisions." This was his way of mocking the common practice of scouts in the NFL, standing like magistrates with stopwatches as prospective draft choices dashed up and down the practice field, forty yards at a clip, in their workout shorts and T-shirts. It was Young's opinion that entirely too much was made of these time trials, that tenths of seconds of foot speed by men in their briefs didn't mean anything if you couldn't measure a player's heart and commitment through his game armor.

Perhaps nobody ever proved Young's point better than Jerry Rice. Coming from Mississippi Valley State in Division IAA in 1985, Rice's records were already suspect to many savvy scouts. The fact that he caught twenty-four passes in one game, or that in another game he caught a dozen passes and scored three touchdowns in the first quarter alone, seemed almost surreal. So, when Rice ran a 4.6 forty, the conventional wisdom was solidified that he was a slow, small-college statistical showoff who couldn't cut it in the NFL.

Only Bill Walsh of the 49ers looked sufficiently at Rice's hands and his hips and not just at his feet. San Francisco came to the draft as Super Bowl champs, with the last pick in the first round. Walsh bundled up his first three choices and traded them to the New England Patriots for their first pick, Rice—number sixteen.

As it was, Rice was still the third wide receiver selected, but it was immediately apparent in the 49ers camp that Walsh's reputation for genius was reaffirmed. Dwight Clark, a veteran 'Niner receiver, watched Rice in awe the first time he worked out. "What is that?" he asked Walsh. Very quickly the team understood how delusionary underwear time trials could be. Ronnie Lott, another of Rice's teammates, announced mysteriously, "Jerry's got game speed. It's hard to explain, but nobody outruns Jerry in a game."

PRIZE HANDS
JERRY RICE

★

When he was in high school, scouts doubted Jerry Rice's ability. Though he set eighteen NCAA records at Mississippi Valley State, many NFL teams thought he lacked the size and speed to be a pro. So Rice worked out daily following his senior season preparing himself for the "next level."

Jerry Rice, watching his San Francisco Forty Niner defense at work

Notwithstanding, Rice's nerves at first rattled. What he could catch in practice, he dropped so often in games that Joe Montana, the 49ers magnificent quarterback, would stand and glare at the rookie as the boos rained down. It wasn't until the fourteenth game of the season, a Monday night national show against the Los Angeles Rams, that it suddenly all came together and Rice caught ten passes for 241 yards. Thereafter he rolled, so that eventually he would accumulate historic numbers: the most receptions and yards for a receiver and the most touchdowns for any player who ever played in the NFL.

Incredibly, at the age of thirty-five, only after a dozen NFL seasons plus seven more in high school and college, did Rice finally miss a game. He endured two serious knee injuries in that year—1997—but he committed himself by returning to the game and enduring two grueling rehabilitations, and when he returned the next season he caught another eighty-two passes. Four years later, still going strong, he joined the Oakland Raiders and put up the same sort of numbers at the age of forty.

Obviously, Jerry Rice has remained wonderfully fit. He is also recognized for his disciplined devotion, perhaps most reminiscent of another practice-slow, game-quick receiver from a different era: Raymond Berry of the Baltimore Colts. "That work ethic is what makes Jerry Rice so special," John Madden said. "He's not only better than any of the other wide receivers, he works harder than any of the others. You don't see that combination too often, where the guy that's the best is also the guy that works the hardest."

And the catalyst that first ignited such commitment? Like many of great character, Jerry Rice had discovered treasure in a setback. When he was in high school in Crawford, Mississippi, he was caught playing hooky in the tenth grade and "punished" by the principal, who made the truant join the football team. Coming from a poor family in a small, impoverished town in the poorest state in the country, Rice found his life changed by that benign sentence. But the rest of his fate was his own doing. ★

★

Just as he has stayed with his career through injuries and in spite of the doubts of others, Jerry Rice has committed himself to a number of charitable causes. But he won't lend his name alone to a program. "For it to work for me I have to commit myself as well as money and my name—I have to be hands-on."

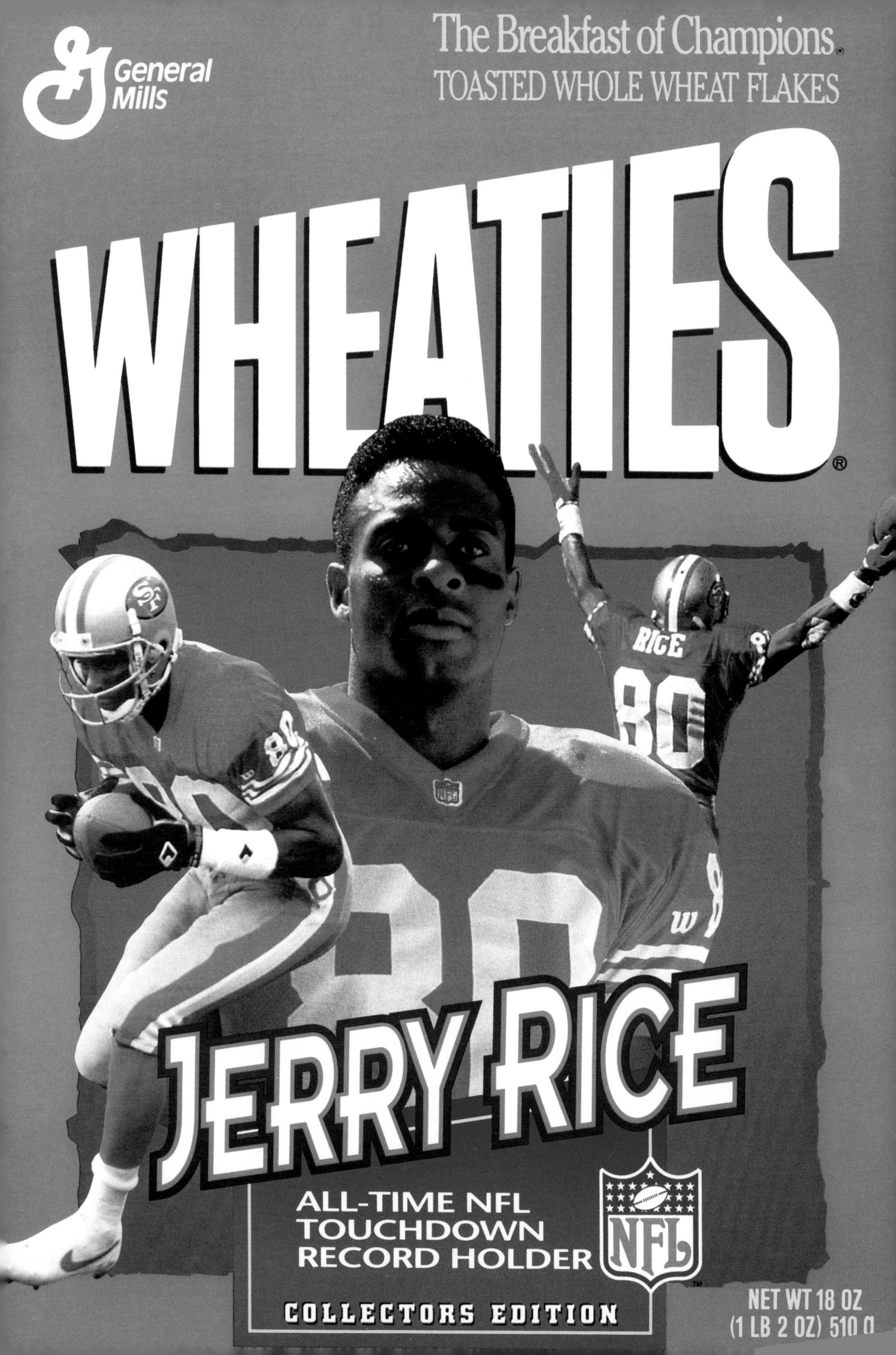

The Breakfast of Champions
TOASTED WHOLE WHEAT FLAKES

WHEATIES

JERRY RICE

**ALL-TIME NFL
TOUCHDOWN
RECORD HOLDER**

NFL

COLLECTORS EDITION

NET WT 18 OZ
(1 LB 2 OZ) 510 g

His mother, Tida, once said, "Tiger has Thai, African, Chinese, American Indian, and European blood. He is the Universal Child." He shot a forty-eight for nine holes when he was three. His father, Earl, compared him to Gandhi when he was barely twenty-one. Hardly older today, and almost everyone agrees that he is the greatest golfer of all time. Maybe Babe Ruth, maybe Wayne Gretzky, maybe Michael Jordan, dominated their sports more for several years, but unless something extraordinary and unforeseen develops, who is to say that Tiger Woods will not become, undisputed, the most awe-inspiring athlete of all?

Tiger Woods, right, and his father, Earl, at a youth benefit event in 2001

Then again, maybe he is already that. Surely, success will never spoil him. After all, although he was the youngest of prodigies, incredibly successful all his life, victory only seems to build in Woods a thirst for more. Tales of his concentration are already legend. He expects to win every tournament. "Tiger can play in Jack's [Nicklaus] style, waiting for his chance," Arnold Palmer said, "or he can play my style, attacking all the time. That's some combination."

EYE OF THE TIGER
TIGER WOODS

In fact, to catalog Woods's array of achievements is to diminish them by the sameness of their excellence, the repetition of glory, the excess of victory. Youngest this, lowest that, most whatever, and so on. But, distilling from only the very best: that first Masters victory at twenty-one; youngest man to win a career Grand Slam; second man (after Ben Hogan) to win three of the four majors in one year; first golfer to hold all four major titles at one time. And then: winning six tournaments in a row; earning more than nine million dollars in a year while averaging 68.17 per round; winning a U. S. Open by fifteen strokes, the most ever in a major tournament. (That broke a record set 136 years ago, which is another record for record-setting.)

Incredible as it seems, he expects to get better. After he won the Masters in 1997, he took time off and rebuilt his whole swing because he perceived a weakness at short irons. This was like tearing down the Taj Mahal and rebuilding it because the doorknobs were a bit loose. Even though he became one of the longest hitters in the history of the sport as a teenager, he put on another forty pounds of muscle and became longer still. How much better can he get?

The answer to that lies in the depth of Tiger's commitment to the game. Clearly, it is a mark of character to respond to failure by discovering the lessons to be learned from adversity and making the effort to change and to improve where needed. But, as in Tiger's case, to respond to successes beyond what most golfers achieve in a lifetime by making major adjustments in his game is a measure of commitment to excellence and self-improvement that bodes ill for his opponents.

Tiger's success has also had a social significance. Since he burst onto the scene, the number of African-American golfers has increased by more than a third, and his youth and verve have changed the whole attitude and sensitivity at the golf tournaments he enters, providing a happier, fresher image for the grand old game. Certainly, Woods's competitors are sharing in his boom. Prize money has tripled during Tiger Time, and, although television ratings have generally been down for most sports, they have doubled during this period for the PGA.

Shortly after Nicklaus first began to dominate the game, the great Bobby Jones generously observed that "Jack plays a game I am not familiar with." By that standard, Tiger Woods plays a game that ventures into the unknown. He remains, however, very much a purist in its finest tradition. His demeanor has been so impeccable that when a microphone caught him spouting a rather predictable angry word after he unleashed a bad drive at one U.S. Open, it was an outright shock to many fans. After all, it was already generally accepted that the Universal Child had grown into the Faultless Man. Not so. Tiger is human, and his success is an example to all us humans of how far we might go when we really commit ourselves to something. ★

Away from the headlines of the Masters and the U.S. Open, Tiger is also committed to helping others. He works with disadvantaged youth through the Tiger Woods Foundation, which promotes minority participation in golf and other activities.

Tiger Woods and Xavier Schmidt in 1999

General Mills

WHEATIES

Grand Slam

TIGER WOODS

CHAMPION

...as been a part

...olf since, as a

...e putted

...e on a 1978

...He was the

...nal magazine

...of five.

...gy has been

...for him,

...s shown

...on

...onstant

...ve.

THERE WERE ONLY two days that really mattered in Bruce Jenner's public athletic life—July 29 and 30, 1976, in Montreal, Quebec, Canada. There he would seek the Olympic decathlon gold medal. He was primed to triumph, but, win or lose and, twenty-six years old, he was never going to compete again. Everything was pointed toward those two days. Four days before the competition he said casually, but very prag-

Bruce Jenner at the U.S. Olympic Trials, 1976.

matically, "I do know if I win and handle myself well, I can work off it for years and years."

And he did. All of the above. He won. He handled himself well. And he worked off it. Jenner has been as versatile in his after-Olympic life as he was in the decathlon. He has been a motivational speaker, an actor, a TV host, an endorser, a water-skier, an auto racer, and any number of other things that have popped up. The decathlon is the art of being pretty good in lots of things, and, in a way, that is how Jenner has lived his life. He also said as much just before his competition in Montreal: "Our whole society is based on specialists. The decathlon goes against that. A decathlon is a presentation of moderation."

MAN OF DESTINY
BRUCE JENNER

Perhaps above all, Jenner has always known himself and his limits. When he graduated from high school in Newtown, Connecticut, only one college wanted him: little Graceland, in Iowa. Although he had been a classic high school athletic hero, Jenner had also been an indifferent student. His problem, finally diagnosed, was dyslexia. Pressure in competing for the gold medal in the Olympics? "The greatest fear of my life," he said, "was having to stand up to read in front of my class as a young kid." But he also credited the dyslexia for inspiring him. First, his embarrassment in the classroom encouraged him to concentrate on sports. Then, as he overcame his learning deficiencies, he was even more determined to succeed.

Once Jenner was introduced to the decathlon by his coach at Graceland, he embraced the challenge with open arms, and his private athletic quest really began. The first decathlon he ever saw was the first he participated in, in 1970. A mere two years later he

★

When first diagnosed with dyslexia while in junior high, Bruce Jenner asked his parents, "Am I going to die from this?" Jenner says the biggest problem dyslexics face is not the inability to perceive words but rather a distorted perception of themselves.

Jenner with the Olympic gold medal, July 30, 1976.

made the U.S. team, and in the Munich Olympics he finished tenth. Three years after that, he set the world record with 8,524 points. He kept a hurdle in the small $145-a-month apartment where he and his first wife, Chrystie, lived in northern California; he sometimes slept with his discus. Chrystie supported them as a flight attendant; they drove an ancient VW bug. Everything in Bruce Jenner's life depended on those two days in July 1976. It was, very simply, "my destiny." He was carving that destiny every day he got up, however sore from the day before, to put in another grueling round of training.

Boyishly handsome, glib, with a wonderful smile, Jenner was described as "Prince Valiant, with muscles." Behind the smile was a singular focus and drive that renewed itself with each small success. When the time came, he had already passed the true test of a champion. In the Olympic stadium on two grim, gray days, Jenner went on to set personal records in five of the disciplines—long jump, shot put, high jump, 400 meters, and 1,500 meters—while equaling his career best in the 100 and the pole vault. He did not waver from what he knew he had to do, and if he did not actually take the lead in the complicated decathlon scoring until the eighth event, he knew all along that the gold was his if he merely scored to his potential.

In the grueling finale, the 1,500-meter run, he outright sprinted the last 300 meters, breaking his own world record. Then he took a flag from a well-wisher and waved it joyously. Although the ritual would soon become common, it was a new victory procedure in 1976. But it was all in good fun, and Jenner was happily accepted by his nation; *Sports Illustrated* characterized him as "bicentennial government issue." When he checked out of his hotel after the Olympics had ended he didn't even take his vaulting poles with him. Instead, off he went to the challenges of the other decathlon of the rest of his life. ★

★

Bruce Jenner used adversity to make his life better. He believes his learning problems in elementary school spurred him to become a great athlete. "Athletics is where I excelled," he said recently. "But where it has really helped me in life is as a father. A good parent understands what his child sees."

THE IRONY PILED upon the tragedy of Dale Earnhardt's death is that the attention paid him, in grief, astonished most Americans who had never heard of him. At that time, February 2001, NASCAR had moved out of its Dixie niche, but for all its burgeoning popularity it remained a sport with little crossover. In large pockets of sophisticated America, the most accomplished, most popular, most controversial driver simply didn't exist.

He was forty-eight years old, had won every race, been given every honor; he had absolutely nothing left to prove. Still, Earnhardt kept on driving, giving no more quarter than he had when he first started on dirt tracks, racing for grocery money to feed his family. In spite of many injuries he seemed inviolate, and had he but lived two more months he would have driven in his record 656th straight race.

THE INTIMIDATOR
DALE EARNHARDT

★

The son of famed short-track champion Ralph Earnhardt, Dale, shown at right spotting for his son Kerry at a race days before his death in the 2001 Daytona 500, took delight in the racing careers of sons Dale Jr. and Kerry. "I'm glad I can watch them doing what I love," he said.

He came from racing territory—Kannapolis, North Carolina—and from racing stock. His father, Ralph, had himself been a top NASCAR driver. Dale dropped out of school after the ninth grade to race. Oddly, however, despite all that he brought to the track and all that he would be, the young Earnhardt had to struggle mightily. His first two marriages failed as he devoted himself to his racing dreams. As late as 1975, when he was twenty-three, he had to roll over small ninety-day notes to pay the bills; finally, in desperation, he joined the boilermakers union.

But then suddenly it all clicked. In 1979 he made Rookie of the Year on the Winston Circuit. The next year he won the championship, and with his give-no-quarter style, the man with the handlebar mustache driving the number three black Chevy was soon the Intimidator, almost as much myth as master. His racing style may have been intimidating, but it also required the courage any driver must have to drive a car in a pack at 180 miles an hour. At the Valleydale 500 at Bristol in 1985 Earnhardt's power steering went out early in the race. Bristol is a short track—tight turns, a lot of shifting and braking and hard steering—and driving without power steering

Dale Earnhardt, center, and sons Dale Jr., left, and Kerry, right, at the 2000 Pepsi 400, Michigan Speedway.

is, in the words of another driver, "like having some-one sit next to you and pull the wheel in the opposite direction." It would have meant an early end to the race for most drivers. Not for Earnhardt. He ran the whole race, and won. By the end, he looked like he had been wrestling gorillas for two hours. But he had made a commitment when he climbed into the car, and he was determined to keep it.

Nor did Earnhardt's sense of commitment end there. In his early days racing for Richard Childress, Dale continued to show that his level of grit and talent were above the rest, even if the cars he was given to drive weren't. Childress, knowing he couldn't put Earnhardt in competitive cars just then, told him he didn't want to hold him back and opened the door for Dale to take a better offer when it came along. "Let's give it some time," Dale said. "We'll do okay."

He would win seven championships in all, and only his oh-for-nineteen shutout at the Daytona 500 marred his record. In 1990 Earnhardt had the race won until his car ran over a small bit of debris and ground to a halt just a turn short. "It's not the Daytona 499," he sighed. When he finally did take the premier NASCAR race in 1998 it was an incredibly popular victory, destiny late but destiny due.

Like the dashing Southern counterpart to whom he was compared—Confederate cavalry General Jeb Stuart—Earnhardt died a hero too young, with his boots on. History will see him as a connecting figure. Earnhardt came to NASCAR when it was still a regional draw. He left it a big-top national show. And, sadly, it was his tragic departure that gave it fame. What he left for the sport he loved was more than just a commitment to winning; it was a commitment to finishing what he started, no matter what the odds. ★

GRACE

GRACE

"With grace of motion that might scarcely seem inferior to angelical . . ." —WILLIAM WORDSWORTH

WE SEE THE beautiful old statues and paintings of the Greeks perfectly poised in their athletic disciplines—most memorably, the perfect symmetry of the discus thrower—taut, beautiful, nude. It all seems so lovely, infinitely more pristine than the raucous smash-mouth competitions that we are used to at the turn of the millennium. But, alas, the beauty of sport has always been menaced by spectacle and by the raw speed and brute strength that can descend into violence.

For all that we celebrate in the races and the javelin tosses of the ancient games, perhaps the most popular event was something called the pankration, which even Plato sneered at as "combining incomplete wrestling with

Don Budge, Wimbledon, July 8, 1937.

incomplete boxing." Which is to say, quite complete mayhem. Ah, but those wonderfully aesthetic Greeks adored the pankration, particularly a champion named Arrikion, who defended his title literally to the death. As Arrikion was being strangled, he won the match by breaking his opponent's toes. Oh, what a lovely war.

So today, even in these allegedly more civilized times, beauty on the field of play invariably plays second fiddle to its grimier qualities. Is there a more telling or awful word in the athletic lexicon than football's *sack?* How telling is the gag, "I went to a fight and a hockey game broke out." The brutish basketball dunk is what we see most in the highlights, not the gracefully arched jump shot.

Yet whenever we can set our barbarous tastes aside, there is nothing as beautiful as watching the best players at play. To begin with, athletes are in the prime of their youth, in the bloom of health, in the pink of condition. If we are indeed formed in God's image, then our sportswomen and sportsmen are the most godlike among us. Too often we acknowledge this only reluctantly. We say, for example, that a double play is "balletic"; why is not a ballet "double-playish"? Art should be a two-way street.

Of course, much of the beauty of sport occurs too fast for us to appreciate. If a Rembrandt flashed by as quickly as Jaromir Jagr crossed the blue line, what could we hope to recall of the Dutch master's craft? So, in sport, we too often admire the result without savoring the craftsmanship.

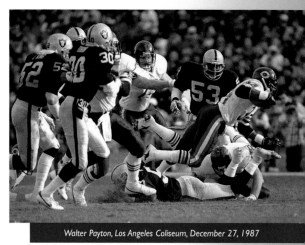

Walter Payton, Los Angeles Coliseum, December 27, 1987

Ted Williams placed in a section titled "Grace" may at first seem jarring. But Williams in the batter's box, balanced, wrists cocked, body tensed, is as finely formed a kinetic portrait as Michelangelo's *David*. Surely, hitting a speeding, spinning baseball with a Louisville Slugger is every bit as graceful as Laurence Olivier intoning Shakespeare or Maria Callas hitting a high note.

There is, in fact, a considerable degree of correlation between grace and success in athletics. In other words, it pays to play pretty. Take, for example, a jockey astride a horse, riding way up on the withers, becoming almost one with the gorgeous beast. Rarely will you see a jockey who is shifting about and flailing in ungainly fashion winning a race. In fact Socrates thought that athletics and aesthetics were equal parts of the whole, that the twin keys to a human being's development were the fine arts and sports. They must merge.

Some sports, of course, are simply more beautiful than others. Indeed, some disciplines, like figure skating or diving, are even sometimes branded as being girlish, too much about sweet and not enough about sweat. But in every game there are many elements of elegance and stylishness. This will elicit howls from soccer fans, but it is certainly possible to postulate that the sport suffers in the American mind because our favored team games are so much prettier to watch. No matter how you slice it, maneuvering a ball with the feet and the noggin lacks graceful proficiency compared to propelling baseballs, footballs, and basketballs with the hands. There is more control in America's games, and, with that, ipso facto, more form. Except possibly when John McEnroe played

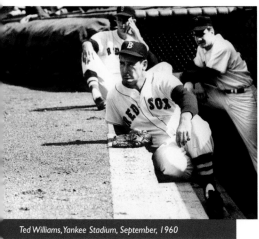

Ted Williams, Yankee Stadium, September, 1960

tennis, beauty has never seemed to flow out of chaos or grotesquerie.

Two developments in sport promise to emphasize gracefulness even further. First, women are entering the lists in greater numbers, and their presence is bound to influence athletics positively even as sport offers them a new direction for growth and fulfillment. And, too, with film to allow us to study athletes, we are sure to dwell more on the beauty of games and of the men and women who play them. That means we don't just see the discus thrower hold the discus; we can see him throw it, which is even more beautiful. ★

STYLES CHANGE, and there are modifications, new materials, sleeker lines, but basically sports uniforms remain remarkably the same. In fact the single most visible revolutionary transformation in sports fashion probably took place in tennis, when men switched from long trousers to shorts during the late 1930s. Maybe that's why the memory of Don Budge remains both so stark and so elegant. The vision of the man and his time is distinct. It wasn't just that he was the last champion to move about the court in long white ducks, gliding across the grass, dominating

Don Budge with U.S. National trophy, September 24, 1938

every element of the game. No, more than that, Budge hit a backhand with such grace and élan (and power) that even now it is still often rated the prettiest stroke the game has ever produced.

There was of course much more to Budge than class. By 1937, on his way to ninety-two straight victories, he so dominated the amateurs (which was the only part of tennis that mattered then) that Budge had to dream up his own challenge to give himself something

GRAND SLAMMER
DON BUDGE

★

Once described as a "civil man in uncivilized times," Don Budge was the consummate sportsman at a time when the world was rushing toward World War II. His 1938 sweep of the championships of Australia, France, England, and the United States represented the first "Grand Slam" of tennis.

to shoot for in 1938. He decided to try to become the first player ever to win the championships of the four countries that had won the Davis Cup—England, the United States, Australia, and France. The Grand Slam, it would be named.

Budge did win his own creation, too, and with such ease that years later, when he recalled that magnificent sweep, he would say (with only a little hyperbole) that the highlight of the year came after he won the French, when Pablo Casals dedicated a private cello performance to the champion.

"That's how I'll always remember Paris," Budge would say. "Señor Casals playing for us, while behind him, out the picture window, there was the city, the Eiffel Tower standing above it all." It wouldn't be long before Paris was burning. More than any other American athlete, Budge is connected to World War II. It isn't just that he played an international game. It isn't just that he injured his shoulder while serving as an officer in the Pacific and would never thereafter be quite so good in short pants as he had been in long. No, most memorable, in 1937, the year before his Grand Slam,

Budge played an international match that has the significance of being called not only the greatest match of all time but also, indisputably, the most dramatic.

The United States was playing Germany, the winner certain to take possession of the Davis Cup. The match was held on the neutral court at Wimbledon, where Budge had won the championship two weeks before, defeating Baron Gottfried von Cramm in the final. And now, in the deciding fifth match of the cup, with Germany and the United States tied at two apiece, von Cramm and Budge prepared to leave once more for center court. The phone rang, and von Cramm was called to answer it. "Ja, mein Führer," Budge heard him say. Hitler himself had phoned to exhort von Cramm to beat the American and bring the cup to Berlin.

The match itself was no less fantastic, of the highest quality, and tit for tat. Von Cramm finally surged ahead 4-1 in the fifth set, but Budge then gambled, daring to move forward to receive serve. It worked. Taking the ball on the rise, Budge broke, then finally won, 8-6. The cup came back to America. Before long, von Cramm—who hated Hitler—was imprisoned by the Nazis. Budge always felt that had he not come back to defeat the German,

Hitler would not have jailed his great friend and rival.

Budge was the most popular of champions, recognized as the ultimate sportsman. It's revealing that he won one final great victory in 1957, when he was playing the reigning world champion, Pancho Gonzales, and Gonzales began the match with a nasty bit of gamesmanship. Gonzales was at the height of his powers, Budge just hanging on, forty-one years old. But Gonzales's antics so infuriated Budge that, somehow, he reached back in anger and whipped the champion in straight sets. One last time it was 1938 and Don Budge, in long pants, ruled a world that would never be quite the same. ★

Shown here hitting an overhead winner en route to the 1937 Wimbledon championship, Don learned his tennis on the playgrounds of Oakland, California, while dreaming of a baseball career. He said his famous backhand was the product of his baseball swing.

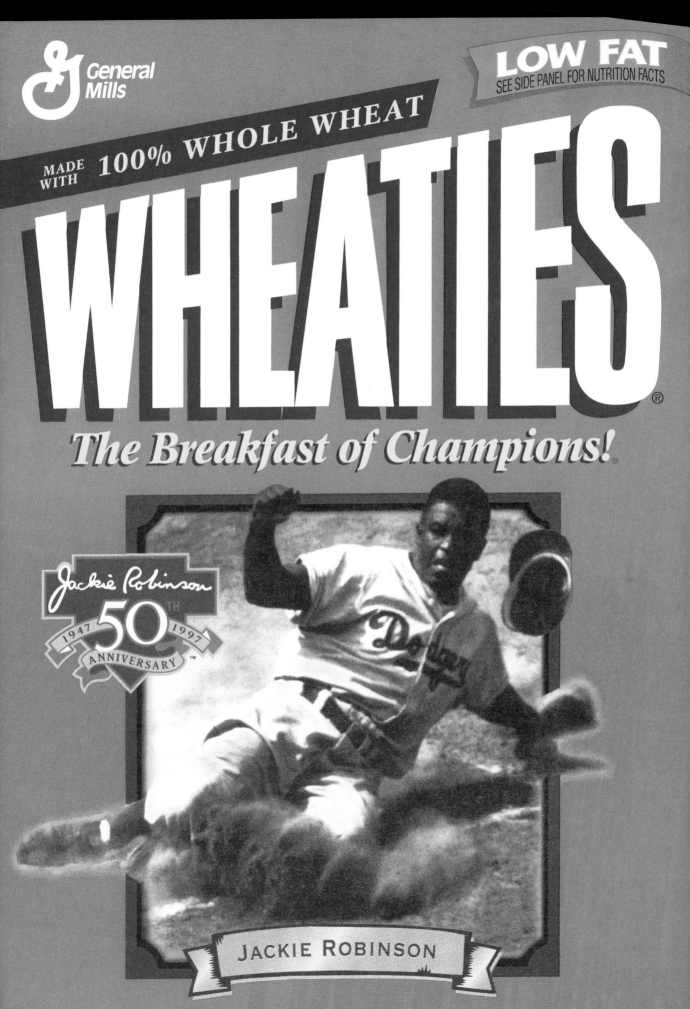

Jackie Robinson has been, indisputably, the single most important athlete in our culture. Lest it be forgot, he may also have been our finest athlete. Baseball was even something of an afterthought. He had been an All-American running back at UCLA, nearly as good as a basketball guard; had there been no war, Robinson would almost surely have won the long jump at the 1940 Tokyo Olympics that were cancelled. Then it was the war—and racism—that triggered a series of events that nudged him into baseball and from there, headlong into history.

In 1943, as a lieutenant at Fort Hood, in Texas, serving in a division that would soon ship out to participate in what would become D Day, Robinson refused a bus driver's command to move to the back of a bus. Although court-martialed, he was exonerated at his trial, but by then his troops had departed for Europe and he was mustered out. Posted briefly to Kentucky to await his discharge, Robinson met another African-American, who had played baseball in the Negro Leagues, and with that chance contact and no other immediate prospects, he signed on with the all-Black Kansas City Monarchs.

A LIFE THAT MATTERS
JACKIE ROBINSON

★

The son of a sharecropper and grandson of a slave, Jackie doubted he was the right man when he was selected to be the one to break baseball's color barrier. Although baseball may have been only Robinson's third-best sport, Jackie clearly had the strength of character that would prove necessary.

So Robinson was there the next season when Branch Rickey, the general manager of the Brooklyn Dodgers, sent Clyde Sukeforth on a scouting mission to select the one Black player who could best break organized baseball's color line. Robinson's subsequent meeting with Rickey, as Rickey portrayed racist fans and players screaming ugly epithets at Robinson, has entered the folklore. "Mr. Rickey, are you looking for a Negro who is afraid to fight back?" he finally asked in exasperation. "No, Robinson," Rickey snapped. "I'm looking for a ballplayer with guts enough not to fight back."

And despite his naturally fiery temperament, Jack Roosevelt Robinson proved he could be that Negro, that ballplayer. After a season in Triple A, he entered the majors in 1947, where he made Rookie of the Year as a first baseman. To succeed, he had to overcome problems with some of his

WHEATIES
now come to you
BETTER. CRISPER. FRESHER
More Delicious Than Ever!

"Breakfast of Champions"

own teammates, palpable hatred from many opponents—one team even threatened to strike if he played—and a deluge of vituperation and threats from spectators. But he survived and thrived, and within a couple of years, as other Blacks joined him in the majors, as Robinson was allowed to be his own true self on the field, he became even more explosive as a player. Now a second baseman, Robinson brought verve and excitement—even intimidation—to every element of his game. Voted MVP in 1949, he would be a first-round ballot Hall of Fame choice after he retired in 1956. To think that Robinson achieved all this knowing, as Spike Lee remarked, that if he failed "it's going to set my people back twenty years," makes his achievements even more amazing.

It may be difficult to appreciate now how significant an American figure Robinson became. As Henry Aaron pointed out, "Even some Black ballplayers don't have a clue" who Robinson was. There had been a few prominent African-American athletes before Robinson, notably Joe Louis, the heavyweight champion, but in 1947 baseball was indisputably the national pastime, the only professional team sport of any consequence. Quickly, Robinson became an iconic figure not only to his whole race, but he also had a telling effect on whites. As prominent as Louis had been, alone in the ring, Robinson was part of a team, playing with white men, representing a whole community. He was, one observer noted, "an Eleanor Roosevelt in spikes." Whereas the North was not legally segregated then, and even prided itself on its fellowship, tacit segregation widely existed. As Rachel Robinson, his widow, says: "Jackie heightened awareness. So many white people were simply oblivious to what was going on around them. Sometimes, you know, indifference is the most pernicious attitude you try to fight."

Robinson never let people ignore him or what he believed in; he fought to the end of his short life, succumbing to diabetes in 1972, when he was only fifty-three. Often, in fact, he took unpopular positions. "Oh, yes," Mrs. Robinson says. "Jackie could be very irritating to people." Freed to be himself, he was unafraid. Most of all, Jackie Robinson mattered. ★

★

The modern era in base-ball didn't begin with Babe Ruth. It began the day Jackie Robinson broke into the major leagues and played his first game with the Brooklyn Dodgers. The dignity with which he endured the taunts and insults from fans and other players helped transform the game.

33 USA

Jackie Robinson

1999

Robinson was a daring base runner who used his quick timing to steal home three times during his rookie year. The excitement he brought to the game with his hitting, skillful bunting, and speed soon made him a household name, but although the taunts were quieter, they were always there. By 1949, however, there were already songs written about him.

THE MOST EVOCATIVE nickname ever in sport surely was "Sweetness." His Chicago Bear teammates hung it on Walter Payton soon after his arrival. Somewhat earlier, in 1703, Jonathan Swift had written, "Instead of dirt and poison, we have chosen to fill our hives with honey and wax, thus furnishing mankind with the two noblest of things, which are sweetness and light." And perverse as it may seem to suggest that any football player could be sweet, Sweetness of the Bears brought light, too, to his space, inside and beyond the sideline stripes.

At Soldier Field in Chicago, as the seconds ticked down on his last game after thirteen seasons, a woman's voice somehow rose above the crowd: "We love you, Walter." Then, in the cold dusk, as he left the field for the last time, the whole crowd chanted simply, "Wal-ter . . . Wal-ter . . . Wal-ter . . ." until he disappeared down the tunnel to meet with the press. "The bottom line is," Payton said at the time, "God blessed me. I've truly been blessed."

Walter Payton, Chicago, December 20, 1987

It was not so easy to say that, however, in the beginning of his life—as of course it would not be at the end. Payton was born poor in segregated Mississippi. There were no big-time colleges calling, so he attended all-Black Jackson State.

SWEETNESS
WALTER PAYTON

★

At a time when many NFL players took to creating dances to celebrate touchdowns and taunt beaten rivals, Walter Payton, the greatest runner and touchdown producer the game had ever seen, simply handed the ball to the ref and jogged off the field.

But there his talent was unmistakable and the Bears made him a first-round choice. Still, at only 5-feet-10, with his soft voice and gentle demeanor, Payton never quite looked like what he was: the best all-around back ever to play football. Why, he ran so hard, said one defensive end who tried to tackle him, that "You felt he was going to pull your arms right out of the sockets."

It was not only that Payton retired as the leading rusher in NFL history, but he also caught passes. He ran back punts. He even served as the team's emergency punter, placekicker, and quarterback. He never once, it seems, ran out of bounds and neither did he ever act out of bounds. He would take the ball and run with it, and then he would return to the huddle to get ready to run again. And when he scored one of his 125 touchdowns he would simply, politely, hand the ball to one of his blockers or to the official nearest him.

In spite of his relatively small size, Payton packed a wallop. When he ran sweeps, as he is shown performing here, gaining nine yards against Detroit in 1978, he almost never opted to run out of bounds to avoid a hard hit. He preferred to lower his shoulder and bounce off tacklers. Although he played the game as hard as anyone ever did, he was gracious and humble once the play was over.

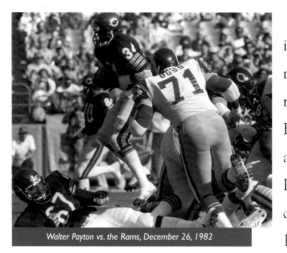
Walter Payton vs. the Rams, December 26, 1982

If Payton suffered one disappointment, it came in the Super Bowl after the glorious 1985 season. For most of Payton's time with the Bears, he set personal records on a poor team with little national exposure. But the fans who saw him knew what he was about and knew what he was worth. "If it wasn't for Walter, I wouldn't be here," read a sign that one fan had draped over the wall in the end zone on a bitter day late in yet another losing season. Slowly, however, the Chicago Bears began to come around, and the 1985 club became not only a winner but a national fancy. The players even had their own song-and-dance video.

They lived up to their reputation in the Super Bowl, too, whipping the Patriots 46-10. But for Payton, in his one championship appearance, it was a most pedestrian afternoon. He gained only sixty-one yards on twenty carries. Worse, even rather mysteriously, when the Bears had the ball inside New England's two-yard-line three times, three times the ball was not given to Payton. Mike Ditka, the Bears' coach, swore that he had intended no slight, and, typically, Payton hugged Ditka, accepting that explanation without rancor. Tellingly, though, when a reporter suggested that the powerful Bears would surely return to the Super Bowl, that Payton would have his chance to score again, he shook his head. "I keep telling you guys," he said, "tomorrow is promised to no man."

Sadly, the words were foreboding. Only fourteen years later the man who was generally considered as fine a competitor as ever sport had seen, who had missed but one game to injury in thirteen seasons, that good man was dead at the age of forty-five of liver cancer. In his wake he left an indelible memory of explosive strength on the field and of grace when the play was done, as he bounced back to his feet, to pause before turning back to the huddle to help up one of his tacklers. ★

Said Ted Williams in 1939, newly arrived in Boston and soon to be dubbed the "Splendid Splinter" by local sportswriters: "All I want out of life is that when I walk down the street, people will say, 'There goes the greatest hitter who ever lived.'" Some, notably members of the Boston sporting press—"maestros of the keyboard," Williams facetiously called them in his farewell address in 1959—never forgave him such pretension. By then he was not so much a splinter anymore; he was Teddy Ballgame. But, in fact, if Williams hadn't lost so much time to wars and injuries, the statistics would probably have certified his youthful wish.

Ted Williams, left, and Joe DiMaggio, Fenway Park, Boston, August 18, 1942

THE SPLENDID SPLINTER
TED WILLIAMS

★

Tall and angular, Ted Williams had perhaps the most picturesque swing in baseball history. His vision was so acute he could see the spin on the ball quicker than other hitters and therefore knew how it would move. His whole body worked in unison to provide surprising power to that fluid swing.

Certainly he was the most dedicated hitter, refusing to bite at any pitch that his remarkable eyesight judged even a smidgeon off the plate. And as best as the art critics of the diamond can tell us, he was the sweetest-looking hitter. Well, maybe Shoeless Joe Jackson was just as pretty. But Jackson couldn't spin the sugar of his swing into power the way Williams could. The Kid—that doesn't change; he will be the Kid forever—hit both for distance and for average. If the pitch was over the plate, he swung. He was the last man to hit .400, in 1941, when he was twenty-three. And he would have hit .400 in 1958 when he was forty if he could have somehow legged out a measly eight more hits. Okay, so he hit only .388 at forty years old.

Williams's stubbornness cost him dearly in matters of affection, however. In his second game in Boston he made an error and was booed. He vowed never again to tip his hat to these picayune fans, and he never did. Twice, in fact, he spit at them. Even on his magical last at bat, September 28, 1960, when he smashed one final glorious home run, the Kid refused to tip his hat. But the vengeful maestros of the press box had had their pound of flesh. Williams would have surely won not three but five or six Most Valuable

Ted Williams in the cockpit of an F9F-5 Panther jet, September, 1952

Player awards had not some writers willfully withheld their votes because of their personal animus against him. The Boston writers generally poisoned the public mind as well, painting Williams as a selfish creature who cared only for his own glory.

To be sure, he was not an outstanding fielder, but the only real blotch on the Williams legend were ten crucial games in the late 1940s when he hit poorly in the clutch. He batted a mere .200 in his only World Series, in 1946, and was no more effective in 1948 and 1949 against the Indians and Yankees in end-of-the-season showdowns that cost the Sox two pennants. His critics never forgave him that, just as they never credited him with the drumroll of clutch hits or his unflinching commitment to his nation and to charity through the years.

But Williams was one of those rare athletes (Muhammad Ali is another) whose public reputation changed after his playing career ended. Maybe his proud, unforgiving personality better fit a later time. Appreciation of his service as an air force pilot, which cost him four seasons in World War II and another in Korea, grew, and his dedication to a children's cancer fund cast him more in benevolence than surliness. What once might have been perceived as arrogance came to be seen, with the passage of time, as a most attractive passion. And who could

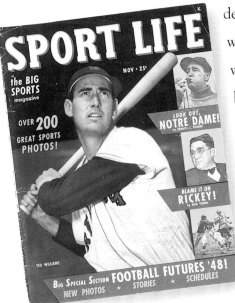

deny Williams as an avatar of excellence? It has been said, with just a hint of hyperbole, that he was the only person in the world who was the absolute best at three things: hitting a baseball, piloting a jet plane (John Glenn was his wingman in Korea), and casting a fly rod.

His reputation as the Grand Old Man of baseball was certified at the 1999 All-Star game in Boston when the current stars of the sport gathered round him like little children before Santa Claus. It was the most affecting of sports scenes. And in Boston, by then, they had named a tunnel after the Kid; he was, in the end, beloved. ★

★

Williams never sat out his duty. He played the last doubleheader of the 1941 season even though by doing so he risked dropping his batting average below .400. He took time out to fight in two wars, and he also helped establish the Jimmy Fund benefiting crippled children.

General Mills
CRUNCHY WHOLE
THE BREAKFAST OF CHAMPIONS
WHEATIES®
WHEATIES CHAMPIONS
AWARD WINNER
Chris Evert Lloyd
NET WT 12 OZ (340g)

ON THE COURT she was, as the British tagged her, the "Ice Lolly." By her own accounting, three out of every four matches she won could be credited to her concentration, and considering that Chris Evert won 1,309 matches, a record 90 percent of those she played, that is a powerful affirmation of mind over matter. Even her own mother nicknamed her "Hiddy," short for "Hideous Creature," which Mrs. Evert dubbed her precisely because she wasn't that at all. To almost everybody, in fact, Christine Marie Evert seemed almost infuriatingly perfect, a monochromatic baseline machine that fired back every shot that dared come her way.

Chris Evert, left, French Open champion, and Martina Navratilova, June 1975

In fact, Chris Evert has always been very human. She possessed a wonderful sense of humor and could even be a little naughty. As Billie Jean King noted, Evert charmed reporters by invariably "inserting sex into a press conference in a very coy way." See what the boys in the back room will have. Moreover, for all her vaunted ability to focus, even her two-handed backhand could be stilled by a fluttering heart. In 1975 at Wimbledon, leading King 3-0 in the third set, Evert glanced up into the stands and saw Jimmy Connors, her old boyfriend, sitting with a beautiful actress. She promptly fell to pieces and lost the match. At Wimbledon three years later, when she had just fallen hard for the handsome British player, John Lloyd, Evert lost a tough three-set final to Martina Navratilova yet seemed almost devil-may-care afterward. "If you've ever been in love," she explained, "you'll know how that match didn't mean all that much to me."

But day in and day out, Lord, how the Ice Lolly hated to lose! The grand rivalry with Navratilova extended for eighty matches over almost sixteen years, but to Navratilova the only unattractive feature of her rival's makeup was a constitutional inability to admit defeat. Except in the most extreme circumstances, Evert would maintain that she had not been beaten; rather, she had simply played poorly.

And so, cute and fetching as she was, her grit was obvious to anyone the instant she burst onto the scene.

CHRISSIE
CHRIS EVERT

★

Feminine, athletic, and relentless, Chris Evert not only revolutionized women's tennis with her two-handed backhand, she raised the game to new levels of public awareness. Soon after her first appearances on center court, millions of waifs across the land were hitting those "two-fisted" backhands.

Chris Evert at the U.S. Open in Flushing Meadows, September 1988

There, at sweet sixteen, in the 1971 U.S. Open, Evert knocked off five seasoned pros in a row, most spectacularly in her national TV debut, beating Mary Ann Eisel, the fourth-ranked American. Eisel had won the first set and was serving for the match at 6-5, 40-0. Unshaken, Evert faced-down six match points, then won the set and the match. In the locker room, the older pros were furious at the precious teen princess who was stealing their thunder. It took Billie Jean King to instruct them in marketing. "Look, she's great for us, great for the game." So she was.

Soon enough, too, Evert had replaced King at the top of the world. By 1974 she would run off a record fifty-five wins in a row and start her collection of major championships. She won eighteen Grand Slam singles all told, but more impressive, she won at least one title from 1974 through 1986—thirteen straight years of championships. No athlete in any major sport has ever achieved such an extended mark of consistency.

And over time, if fans never could quite cherish Evert's steady, wearing style of play, they came to honor the woman holding the racquet. There was always such an honesty to Chris Evert. "I realize a lot of fans think my game is boring," she said, "but this is the game I play to win." So, while consistency may not be pretty, the steady drone of victory is very becoming.

It is instructive that during her career there were a number of outstanding rivalries, and she was always one part of them: Evert vs. King, Evert vs. Evonne Goolagong, Evert vs. Tracy Austin, Evert vs. Navratilova. That last was the epic, of course, a glorious competition that was at once so intense and yet so affectionate that both women and their sport were advanced. "We've seen each other hurt and crying—so vulnerable," Evert would say. "That draws you close." The younger, swashbuckling Navratilova eventually gained the edge after a number of years, but it was the majesty of the rivalry and the mutual respect they shared that ruled above all. ★

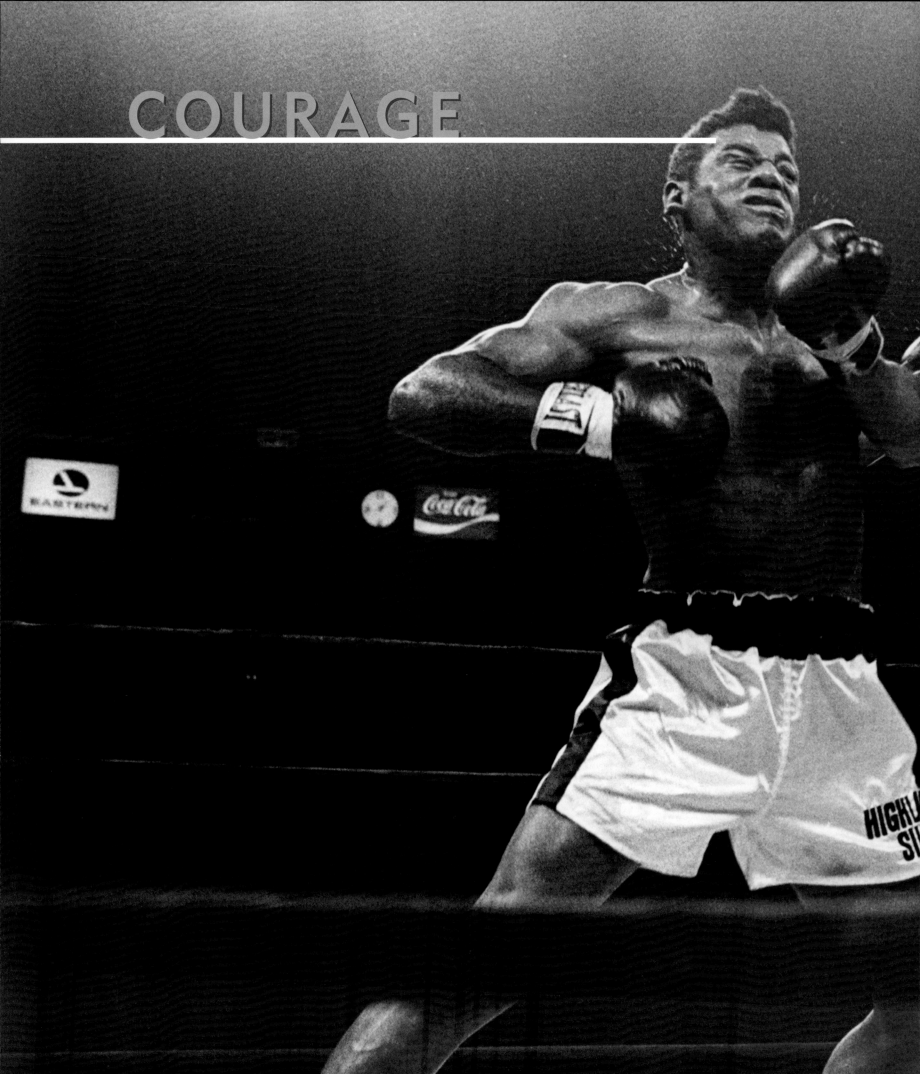

COURAGE

> *"Courage is not simply one of the virtues but the form of every virtue at the testing point."* —C. S. LEWIS

COURAGE

TO BE SURE, it is silly to compare the courage of an infantryman charging a machine-gun nest to, say, a golfer going for the green with a one iron out of the rough. Nonetheless, the more gallant components of humankind may be found in all manner of men and women doing all manner of everyday things. Besides, to praise the emergence of courage on the field of play does nothing to diminish the wondrous actions of those who actually risk their lives.

Courage? To most of us on the sidelines it would take courage enough to enter the ring against someone like Joe Louis, or to buckle up behind the wheel of a race car, or to stand at the plate against the likes of Sandy Koufax. Recall the story of the hitter who came to bat against the fireballing Big Train, Walter Johnson, late one afternoon, lighting a match as he took his stance. "That won't help you see the pitch," said the bemused umpire. "See the pitch?" replied the player. "I just want to make sure Johnson sees me."

No, courage dresses in all sorts of clothes, and for the many athletes who have exhibited it fearlessly under pressure in a tight game with everything on the line and the world watching, there have also been a

Donna de Varona, AAU swimming champion

few who have shown the truest colors off the field or outside the confines of the game. Most surely, Jackie Robinson was a man of courage to brave the racists who taunted and threatened him when he broke baseball's color line. And Pee Wee Reese, the Southern teammate who conspicuously stepped over to Robinson and, without a word, placed an arm around his shoulder as the vile insults streamed from the grandstand and the other dugout—that is courage, too. Like it or not—and the majority didn't—Muhammad Ali knew he was forfeiting his title when he refused to be drafted for a war he could not morally countenance. And all-star center fielder Curt Flood sacrificed his whole baseball career by challenging baseball's odious reserve clause.

Likewise, many Blacks and whites alike told Arthur Ashe to stay out of politics—and out of South Africa. "If you go, they're using you," he was warned. "Yes, I know," Ashe replied softly, "but don't you see? I'm using them, too." And simply by walking onto a court in Johannesburg, it was he, the athlete, who took the first unlikely step in the journey that would soon enough march apartheid out of that benighted land.

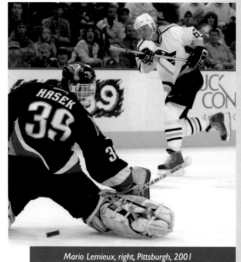
Mario Lemieux, right, Pittsburgh, 2001

But then, in the lighted arena itself, when we talk of "coming through in the clutch" we are really using that casual phrase as a synonym for courage, aren't we? And inelegant as the word may be, to "choke" is to act out of fear, to be the coward. We mask those hard words with softer jargon. Of course in moments of honesty all athletes will admit that sometimes they choke. The trick is just to choke less than most, to find peace and calm in the swirl of the most intense moment. And even then courage alone doesn't ensure victory but allows only for the better possibility.

"Courage," Winston Churchill wrote, "is the greatest of all human virtues because it makes all the others possible." (Remembering his youth, he also wrote, "Nothing is so exhilarating as to be shot at without result," which probably explains why young people are prepared to buckle up into a race car or to strap on skis at the top of a steep mountain or to stand in a net with a hockey puck bulleting toward them.)

Ultimately, as frivolous as our games may seem to be, courage in sport does matter a great deal. Most

Lou Gehrig, Yankee Stadium, July 4, 1939

forms of courage aren't especially visible. Most courage, in fact, is quiet. Often, it is the refusal to do something, and such refusals may happen out of sight, in private moments and hidden places. But still we need to know of courage, to see it on display, so that by visible example we may be emboldened to take a risk ourselves someday. It is fine to hear of the boy who saved his brother from the burning deck, to envision the brave souls holding off the hordes at the Alamo, but, ah, to see the photograph of Johnny Unitas, standing firm, arm perfectly cocked, surrounded by huge invaders who will in a moment pound him into the turf—that is to see courage on the hoof. And with that, at least some small part of us thinks, "Maybe somewhere, maybe once in my life, I too, can . . ." ★

His SKILLS WERE apparent when he was only six, skating in suburban Montreal, besting ten-year-olds. It was all effortless, so much so that he would regularly be accused of loafing even though at every level, from peewee to the National Hockey League, it was child's play for him. He scored a goal in the NHL on his first shift, with his first shot, beating an all-star defenseman and an all-star goalie. All the more commanding that he was handsome and grew larger and stronger than almost everybody else, handling the puck even as he could protect it—some kind of an oversized

Mario Lemieux, No. 66 in white, Chicago, 2000

elf. There was no need even to train. He prepared for each new season, he joked, only "by stopping putting ketchup on my french fries."

Of course, Mario Lemieux's very name means, in his native French, "the best." Everything seemed so easy, so preordained. Why, he and Nathalie, his wife-to-be, even found love at first sight when they met, she all of fifteen, he but seventeen. No one, ever, in any sport, was so much the natural as Mario was in hockey.

SUPER MARIO
MARIO LEMIEUX

★

Although the demands of hockey were easy for Mario Lemieux, there were more difficult trials. Overcoming injuries and disease became a way of life for him. When he returned to the ice on December 27, 2000, after a 3½-year retirement, Lemieux said, "This comeback is the easiest. . . . I'm healthy."

Everybody who has ever seen a movie—or read Aesop's fables or O. Henry or Peanuts—must know that such a perfect life as Mario Lemieux's was too pat. F. Scott Fitzgerald once said there are no second acts in American life. But Mario Lemieux is Canadian, and suddenly, with him, the natural order of things took a difficult turn. He began to suffer terrible back pains, twice had operations, and even when he could play he was facetiously listed as "eighty percent functional, twenty percent pain." A spinal infection kept him out of two-thirds of the 1990–91 season. Not enough? In 1993 he was diagnosed with Hodgkin's disease, a form of cancer that had already killed a cousin. At the height of his powers Lemieux had to walk away from his sport. Besides, his franchise, the Pittsburgh Penguins, in the new hometown that he loved, was going under.

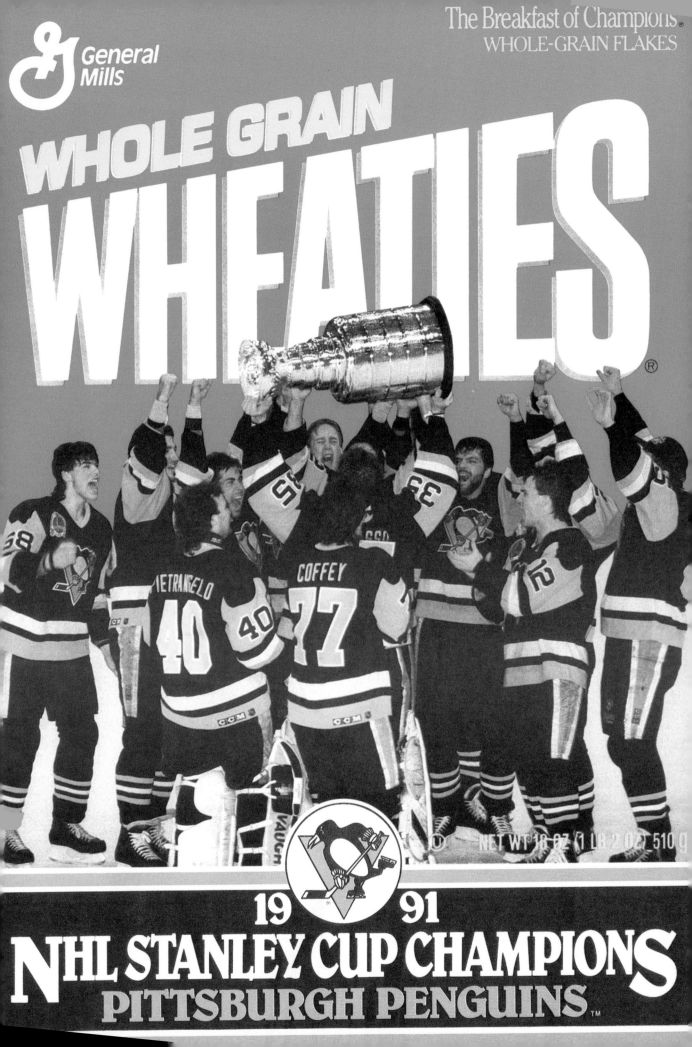

Then his first son, Austin, was born prematurely and at two pounds was unable to leave the hospital.

There remained within Lemieux, however, a reservoir of great strength. A loner by nature, he exhibited the same sort of stalwart resolution in calamity that he had shown so easily in success. He cried for hours when he learned of his cancer, but after that release there was never another tear, let alone so much as a murmur of self-pity. Dave Molinari, the hockey writer for *The Pittsburgh Press*, had turned to Flaubert to best explain the two sides of Lemieux: "Be regular and orderly in your daily life, so you can be violent and

Mario Lemieux, right, and Bob Erray, left, Pittsburgh, May 25, 1991

original in your work." Now the great skater prepared to carry on every day, patiently and steadfastly, in the more commonplace afterlife that had been forced upon him.

Two circumstances conspired to bring him back to the ice after three-and-a-half seasons. First, rather than see the Penguins moved to another city, he saved the franchise for Pittsburgh, buying a significant part of the team himself. The French-Canadian working-class kid with a tenth-grade education was now an American executive. More important, little Austin Lemieux survived and thrived, and his father began to regret that his son had never seen him play. Lemieux began to practice on the sly, then came back to his sport at the age of thirty-five with the same facility he had first shown as a teenager. He rang up a goal and two assists in his first game back. He was in remission only from cancer, not from brilliance. Although Lemieux often had to take games off to spare his back, number 66—*soixante-six*—was a dominant force again.

There were those who maintained that Mario at his best was *le mieux*, the best ever to play the game. Indisputably, he scored goals at a far higher rate than anyone else. Nevertheless, the many seasons lost to his injuries and illness made it impossible for Lemieux ever to surpass Wayne Gretzky as the greatest offensive player in the sport. But in a crude, chaotic game where physical courage is expected, Mario Lemieux displayed something that is never assured, even among the toughest men. No one is naturally valorous, for valor can emerge only from adversity. ★

As if Hodgkin's disease, a spinal infection, and a debilitating back injury weren't crosses enough to bear, Mario Lemieux decided to take it on himself to save hockey in Pittsburgh when the Penguins were nearly broke and on the verge of leaving the city. He not only saved hockey, he returned to play as the first owner-player in modern history.

Lemieux capped his comeback to hockey and realized a dream at the same time when he helped Team Canada win the gold medal in the 2002 Olympics in Salt Lake City. Here he battled Belarus forward Vadim Bekbulatov for position in the corner during the semifinal game. A strong man who never backed down from the challenges of a very physical sport, Lemieux never blinked in his battle with Hodgkin's disease, either.

PEOPLE MIGHT HAVE puzzled at Richard Nixon, but in the end they felt they had figured him out. The same with Clinton or MacArthur or Howard Hughes and all the other enigmas of the last century. But Muhammad Ali? For all we know, for all the movies and books about the man, how little do we really understand him except that he was very, very good at what he did professionally? That, but nothing more.

In 1962 he was young Cassius Clay, a perfectly handsome man (just ask him), constantly babbling, often bizarre. He talked about outer space and the laws of nature as he saw them, all the time drawing spacemen and arrows and circles and God knows what else. He may have been contemplating the beginning of his new spiritual journey, but he was certainly confounding.

Cassius Clay at the gym, 1961

THE GREATEST
MUHAMMAD ALI

★

No one ever questioned his guts when he climbed into the ring. But when he accepted the Muslim faith, changed his name, and then in 1967 refused induction into military service during the Vietnam War, the heavyweight champion became the focal point of conflicting social forces in America.

Forty years later we see an old Ali, heavyset, trembling, barely able to speak, muttering the same old jokes, then suddenly bored, even falling asleep, as those about him chatter on. And yet he seems happy, smiling when his fans greet him, glowing at children, maybe performing the same old magic tricks or passing out a business card for "GOAT—Greatest Of All Time, Inc." But then this, too: Sometimes, out of the blue, he will suddenly flash his feet, doing the old Ali shuffle as sure as if Bundini Brown were there again in his corner and he really were still the Greatest. Ali, it seems, has found contentment even in his infirmity, and he still confounds his audience.

There was, even at the height of his powers, such a child in him. Yet like a child, he could be cruel, sometimes humiliating an opponent with a nickname: the Big Ugly Bear, the Rabbit, the Gorilla. He employed the ugliest racial imagery, somehow knowing that the world would tolerate it even as it would abide it from no other. Yet Ali preached forgiveness and lived principle,

At the age of twelve, young
Cassius Clay had his bicycle
stolen in his hometown of
Louisville, Kentucky. He
took his anger to the gym
and learned to box. Ten
years later, in 1964, he won
the heavyweight championship
from the strongly favored
Sonny Liston, an intimidating
champion who failed to
intimidate Ali, celebrating
here as Liston failed to answer
the bell for the seventh round.

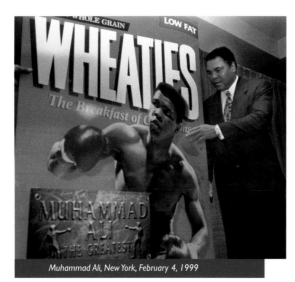

Muhammad Ali, New York, February 4, 1999

as we know, most famously by refusing to be inducted into the Army during Vietnam. "I ain't got nothin' against them Viet Cong," he explained vaguely. It cost him his heavyweight title and his livelihood for four years in his prime until a Supreme Court decision permitted his return to the ring for more magnificent high jinks.

Ali was blessed with the right opponents, starting with Sonny Liston, the ex-con, a glacier of a man. Poor old Sonny; the kid wore him to a frazzle. A decade later George Foreman was supposed to be as indomitable as Liston, and he was attractive and patriotic to boot. But for the Rumble in the Jungle in Zaire, Ali used the "Rope-a-Dope" tactic to wither Foreman on the vine. And Smokin' Joe Frazier may have been the perfect foil, the opposite of Ali in every way. He was a dark, brooding, taciturn presence, perhaps baffled by all the attendant Ali razzle-dazzle. A decent man, Frazier was your basic slugger. "Man," Frazier said after he lost their rubber match, the "Thrilla in Manila," "I hit him with punches that would bring down the walls of a city."

Perhaps nobody knew it then, but those words of praise foreshadowed the future, where Ali would pay for his fearlessness. Before he fought Liston, Ali had asked of his older opponent, "What kind of man can take all those punches to the head?" But as his own end neared, he never inquired so forthrightly about what his own brain could endure. The last battering he took for a payday was from a journeyman palooka when Ali was in his fortieth year.

And then slowly but surely, even as he deteriorated before our eyes, affection for him grew more generous. Perhaps we have finally seen in him what lies beyond the fearlessness and

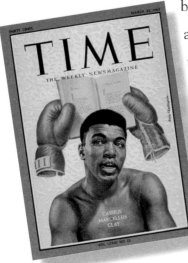

bluster, the grace that is beyond the obvious physical and mental agility the man once had. One raw, cold morning not long ago at the Vietnam Memorial in Washington, D. C., visitors who had made the pilgrimage to find the name of someone they had loved and lost encountered, as well, a familiar figure—Muhammad Ali, he who famously refused to fight in that war. To a person, they hurried over to him and laughed, wanting to see him up close, to say, "Hi, Champ" and maybe even have their picture taken with him. Ali smiled back, trembling, unsurprised. ★

Celebrated on a Wheaties box in 1999, right and upper left, Muhammad Ali's dignity as a retired champion has helped cement his stature as an American hero.

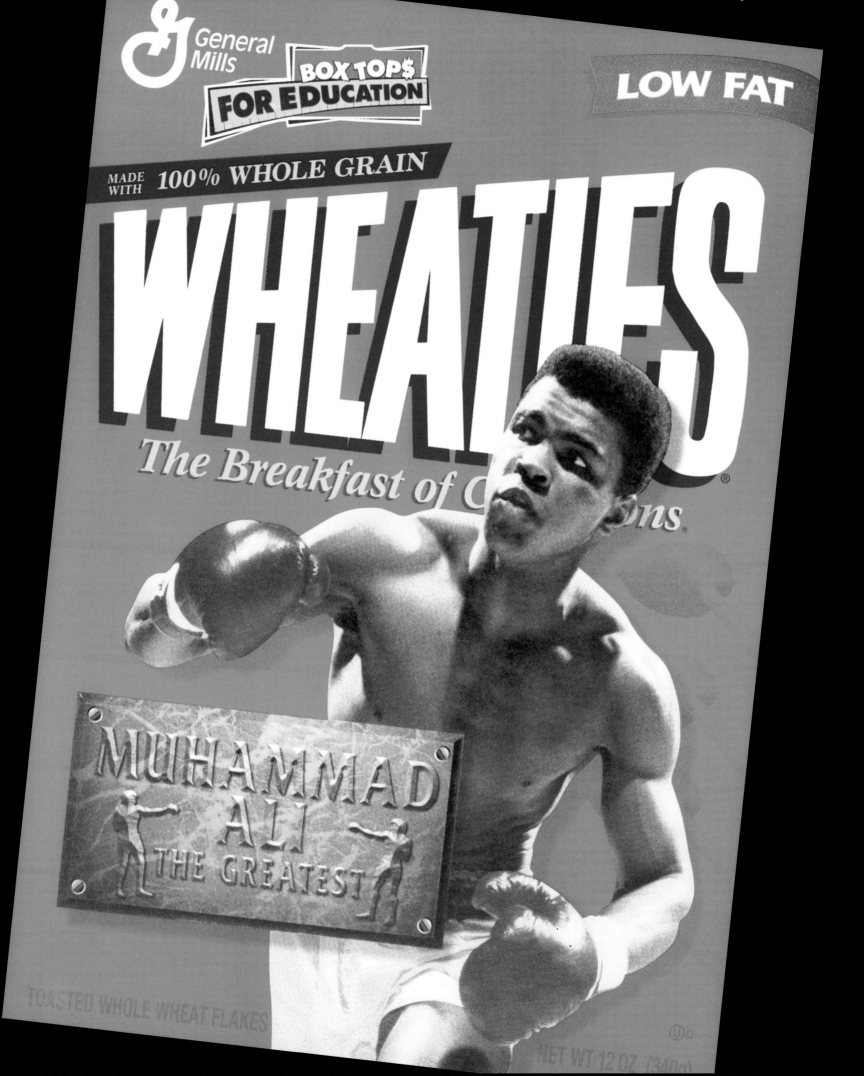

THE IRONY OF Donna de Varona's career is that she was an Olympian at thirteen but a has-been at seventeen, so she spent the next four decades making her mark in the business and the spirit of sport so that no other girl would ever have to suffer her history.

It seems almost ludicrous now, but in 1964, when she was the U.S. Female Athlete of the Year, a double gold medal winner at the Tokyo Games, arguably the most versatile swimmer in history, de Varona was, essentially, forced to quit. "No, I didn't want to," she said. "I knew I wasn't even close to my peak." She was

Donna de Varona, September, 1964

already as famous a female athlete as there was in the country. She had been on the cover of *Life* and *The Saturday Evening Post* and she had twice been the *Sports Illustrated* cover

TRAILBLAZER
DONNA DE VARONA

girl. She'd even written an article for *Life* before the Tokyo games. "That's what I'm here for," she wrote at the conclusion of the piece, "to get that gold medal, boys. . . . Gung ho, guts out." Donna was vivacious, articulate, a fine student—yet not a single college in the United States would tender her an athletic scholarship. Only boys could earn scholarships then.

So de Varona went to college on her own, helping pay her tuition at UCLA by working as a sports reporter for ABC. She was on the air nationally before her eighteenth birthday, on her way to becoming the first full-time female television sports correspondent. De Varona was also appointed to three presidential commissions. She almost surely would have been selected as the first American woman on the International Olympic Committee except that she had established the reputation of being too independent. The IOC wanted women as window dressing, and so they picked someone safer instead.

After de Varona watched Billie Jean King whip Bobby Riggs in 1973, she called up the tennis champion and together they spearheaded the formation of the Women's Sports

★

As sensational as her swimming exploits were, they paled when compared to the opportunities Donna opened for women in athletics. The fruits of this work include thousands of scholarships for female athletes and a marked elevation of the level of skill in all women's sports.

Donna de Varona, Tokyo Summer Olympics, October, 17, 1964

Foundation, which has been crucial to advancing the cause of women in athletics. About the same time, working as a special consultant to the Senate, she played a major role in the passage of the Amateur Sports Act and, perhaps most important, in the passage of Title IX, which effectively brought equality to women in sport. "I'll never forget, after I won my golds but couldn't get a scholarship like all the guys, that what I'd won seemed somehow cheaper," she says. "It was a devastating feeling."

That forced ending of de Varona's competitive swimming crashed a skyrocket of a career. She had been almost eleven years old when she swam in her first race, finishing tenth. Less than three years later, just 5-feet-2 and barely 100 pounds, she was swimming relay on the U.S. Olympic team in Rome. She remembers Walt Bellamy, the 7-foot basketball star, hoisting her up on his shoulders so she could see the opening ceremony. Four years later, grown to 5-feet-6 and filled out to 135 pounds, she was the star in Tokyo. And then, just like that, it was all over. Wrote *The New York Times*, guilelessly, "Swimmers rarely continue long enough to grow old gracefully in their sport, particularly gal swimmers."

In fact, de Varona and whole generations of "gal" athletes were forced to forfeit their best years, and that can never be rectified. De Varona had to content herself with the satisfaction of righting wrongs. In 1999 came a special, bittersweet reward. Her father, Dave, who had called Donna "my little fishie," had been a superb athlete himself, a member of the record-setting University of California crew and an All-American lineman on the undefeated Cal football team that had shut out Alabama, 13-0, before 100,000 fans at the 1938 Rose Bowl.

Sixty-one years later, dying of emphysema, Dave de Varona watched as another 100,000 fans showed up at the Rose Bowl. But this time the throng was there for the finals of the women's World Cup soccer tournament. It was the largest crowd ever to watch a women's sporting event, and the World Cup's chairman was his little fishie. ★

"I will always be an activist . . . that is a lifetime commitment," Donna said. She is a cofounder and the first elected president of the Women's Sports Foundation and, at age nineteen, was a consultant to the U.S. Senate during the drafting of the landmark Title IX legislation that guaranteed women equal opportunities in collegiate athletics.

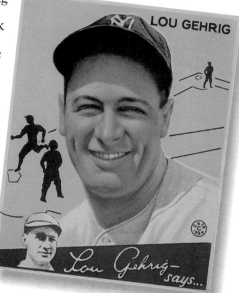

"FOR THE PAST TWO WEEKS," Lou Gehrig said, surely knowing he was dying, "you have been reading about the bad break I got. Yet today I consider myself the luckiest man on the face of the earth." There's no crying in baseball.

So all America would cry for Lou Gehrig. He took himself out of the lineup on May 2, 1939, after 2,130 straight games. He spoke those poignant, wrenching words on July 4, 1939. He died on June 2, 1941. So in the end, although he was one of the greatest baseball players ever, Gehrig is remembered most for getting sick, leaving the lineup, and dying. They named a candy bar after Babe Ruth. They named a disease after Lou Gehrig.

The irony is so obvious it is trite. This great, indestructible rock of a man, 6 feet, 200 pounds, with shoulders big enough to hold up the House That Ruth Built; this quiet, stolid hunk who entered the world at 14 pounds, who played every day through lumbago, back spasms, a broken toe, and (X–rays would reveal) 17 fractures to his great ham hock hands; this steady, reliable

YANKEE PRIDE
LOU GEHRIG

player who averaged more than an RBI a game for eight seasons, who batted above .300 a dozen seasons in a row; this ideal of manly strength and health; this "Iron Horse" wasted away to die, shriveled, before he reached thirty-eight.

Did Gehrig know quite what he was saying when he called himself so lucky? Did he truly believe that? Was he only making it easy for the fans? Preparing himself? Even at his best, he was shy. That day, with 61,000 people awaiting his words, with his teammates, current and past, gathered about him, his manager, Joe McCarthy, had to urge him to step toward the microphone. Then, the "Pride of the Yankees" spoke his brief piece and was gone.

"And silence sounds no worse than cheers/After earth has stopped the ears," wrote A. E. Housman in his poem *To an Athlete Dying Young*. Playing the strong, silent type had never bothered Gehrig, however, and in many

★

So beloved was the victim, that amyotrophic lateral sclerosis forever became known as Lou Gehrig's disease in 1939 after it struck the Yankee superstar in his prime. Baseball's "luckiest man" died two years later.

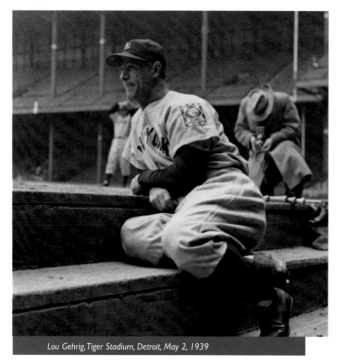

respects he flourished being the junior partner to the ebullient Ruth. The Bambino was already a legend when Gehrig broke into the lineup at first base on June 2, 1925, a fateful sixteen years to the day before he would die. "Do you mind being in the Babe's shadow?" someone asked him after he became a star. "No," Gehrig responded evenly. "It's a pretty big shadow, and it gives me lots of room to spread myself."

Both of the Yankee sluggers were lefties of German heritage—Henry Louis Gehrig was actually christened Heinrich Ludwig—but they had nothing else in common. The playful, boisterous Baltimorean Ruth was the antithesis of the dutiful hometown New Yorker Gehrig, who lived alone with his mother for many years, caring for her until her death.

In their prime together, Gehrig batted cleanup behind Ruth (as he would bat behind Joe DiMaggio in his last seasons), and although Gehrig's achievements were usually a bit less spectacular than Ruth's, in some instances he outshone him. Ruth, for example, never won a Triple Crown as did Gehrig in 1934. Ruth never hit four home runs in a game. Gehrig did that on June 3, 1932, to become the first player in modern baseball to accomplish the feat. Typically, however, he lost the top headline the next morning to John McGraw, who chose that day to retire as the Giants manager after thirty years.

Nonetheless, playing in New York for the fabled Yankees on six world championship teams, Gehrig was hardly ignored. Especially after Ruth left the Yankees at the close of 1934, the Bronx Bombers was Gehrig's team. No one can really know for sure how much pain Gehrig had to endure before his illness became known or how many unexplained symptoms he suffered in silence while playing all those games in a row. But he never whimpered, never stopped enduring until it became obvious that, by keeping on, he would only hurt his team. When his streak was broken by Cal Ripken Jr. it only served to reignite interest in Gehrig. Enough time had elapsed so that his prodigious batting achievements were recalled as much as his dying. And more, the old-timers all remembered his wonderful, gentle smile that had long been forgotten amid the sadness. ★

Although he was one of baseball's all-time greats, Lou Gehrig's record run of 2,130 straight games began in the Babe Ruth era and ended when Joe DiMaggio led the Yankees, meaning the "Iron Horse" usually drew second billing. "I'm not a headline guy," he once said.

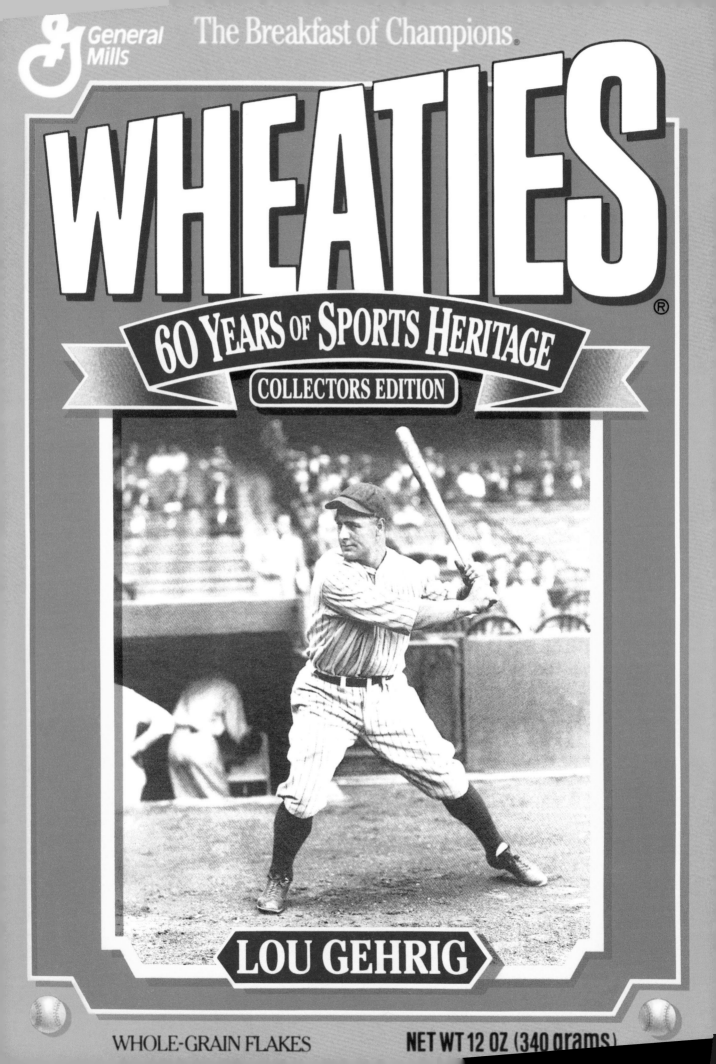

To African-Americans it mattered that Jackie Robinson was not only a Black man but a very dark Black man. To Jewish-Americans it mattered that Hank Greenberg was not only Jewish but a very big Jewish man. When Greenberg became a star with the Detroit Tigers in the 1930s it was a time, Walter Matthau would remember, when every snide joke about a Jew began: "There was this little Jewish gentleman, and . . ." Henry

Hank Greenberg, right, with fellow All Stars, Griffith Stadium, Washington, D.C., July 7, 1937

Benjamin Greenberg was 6-feet-3½, 220 pounds, an especially huge man for that time. That cut down on the ethnic slurs. "You couldn't help but be exhilarated by the sight of one of our guys looking like colossus," Matthau laughed.

Make no mistake: As Robinson would be for Blacks, as Roberto Clemente would be for Hispanics, Greenberg was for Jews—the first prominent major leaguer of that heritage. He wasn't just playing for himself. "I could never just be a bum," he said. "I was always a Jewish bum."

SILENT HERO
HANK GREENBERG

His almost daily battle against anti-Semitism as one of baseball's greatest sluggers wasn't the only stand Hank Greenberg took during his life. His decision to rejoin the army shortly after Pearl Harbor and lose four years of his career to World War II made him a role model for all Americans.

In 1934 it practically became a Talmudic issue: Should Greenberg play games on the High Holy Days in the September pennant race? Finally, as the rabbis debated, Greenberg settled the matter himself, deciding that he would play on Rosh Hashanah, the festive Jewish New Year, but would take off Yom Kippur, the Day of Atonement. Edgar Guest commemorated Greenberg's Solomon-like decision with a poem that concluded:

Come Yom Kippur—holy fast day wide-world over to the Jew
And Hank Greenberg to his teaching and the old tradition true,
Spent the day among his people, and he didn't come to play.
Said Murphy to Mulrooney, "We should lose the game today!
We shall miss him in the infield and shall miss him at the bat,
But he's true to his religion—and I honor him for that!"

The 1930s were ripe with anti-Semitism and Greenberg received some of the ugliest taunting, but never did he let

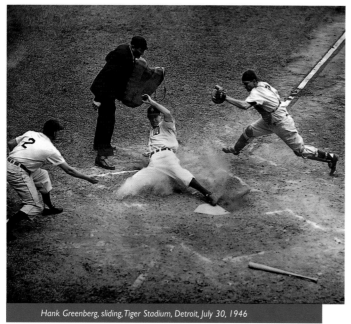
Hank Greenberg, sliding, Tiger Stadium, Detroit, July 30, 1946

his teammates know how wounded he might be. After one particularly vile experience, when some player from the White Sox dugout repeatedly insulted him, Greenberg showed no emotion: He simply went to the Chicago clubhouse after the game and asked for the loudmouth to stand up. No one did. Greenberg confronted each player, face to face, then left, never saying another word about the incident. There was no more heckling from the White Sox, either.

Ironically, Greenberg first had to overcome his own familial confrontations. His parents, Romanian immigrants, thought their son was wasting his life concentrating on sports. "Jewish women on my block would point me out as a good-for-nothing," Greenberg recounted later. "I was Mrs. Greenberg's disgrace." But in 1934, only his second season with the Tigers, he was the American League Most Valuable Player. The next year he drove in 170 runs as Detroit won the World Series, and he rang up 183 RBIs in 1937, a total no one has reached in the sixty-five years since. In 1938 Greenberg had fifty-eight home runs, with five games left to break Babe Ruth's record, but he hardly saw another good pitch to hit. Some claimed the pitchers were determined not to let a Jew gain baseball's most sacred mark; Greenberg never complained, however. "Fifty-eight is not a bad year" was all he said.

Neither did he complain, when, in the spring of 1941 at the age of thirty he was drafted into the army. Greenberg was released as overage on December 5 that year, but, three days later, after Pearl Harbor, he reenlisted, the first major leaguer to volunteer his service. Refusing easy stateside duty, he rose to captain in the air force, flying one of the first missions over Tokyo in 1944. Greenberg lost almost five seasons in the heart of his career. He hit a home run in his first game back.

Retiring after the 1947 season, Greenberg subsequently became the first Jewish owner and general manager in the majors. When he died in 1986 he was remembered foremost as a man of humility and goodwill. He was also recalled as one of the first athletes to charge for his autograph—he gave all the money to Pets Adoption and matched it, dollar for dollar. ★

★

A baseball executive after his playing career ended, Hank Greenberg was back in the moral spotlight in the 1970s when he broke with most of his peers, testifying on behalf of Curt Flood when the outfielder challenged baseball's restrictive reserve clause.

LOOK

AMERICA'S FAMILY MAGAZINE

APRIL 30, 1946 **10¢** 12¢ IN CANADA
YEARLY SUBSCRIPTION $2.50

Evil Over Germany
By GEORGE BIDDLE

1946 World Series Preview

Hank Greenberg
(PAGE 50)

HY PESKIN PHOTOGRAPH

TEAM EFFORT

"Talent wins games, but teamwork and intelligence win championships."—MICHAEL JORDAN

TEAM EFFORT

AS INDIVIDUALISTIC AS Americans are supposed to be, the concept of team is probably more instilled in U.S. athletes than in those of any other nationality. After all, in most countries there is only one major team sport—and that of course is soccer. But in the United States we change our seasons with team sports—football in the fall, basketball in the winter, baseball in the spring. Hockey is also prominent in some areas, and a number of other team games, such as lacrosse and volleyball and soccer itself, also enjoy popularity. Both as players and spectators, we are inundated with team games.

American children learn not only to play several team sports, but because athletics are so widespread in our educational system, school teams in the United States are an integral part of our everyday lives. From early on we get used to the expectation that we will go out for the team. Do we ever hear anything more joyous than "You made the team!"? The emphasis on school sport may be undesirable in some respects, but that very focus teaches children the value and rewards of the team from an early age.

The U.S. and Soviet hockey teams, 1980

It is worth speculating, too, how much the team ethic will be advanced now that girls are enjoying the same opportunity to play on teams as boys have always had. Until recently, most high-profile athletics for girls have been individual sports, but now that women's basketball, soccer, and softball have begun to gain prominence the effect for women growing up and learning team games is bound to have considerable influence on our whole society.

Of course, the team is always in conflict with the individual. Whereas the best coaches in individual sports are usually marked by a talent for teaching function and technique, the best team coaches are, invariably, evangelists more than professors, who can instill common group values, who can convince players to sacrifice self.

Tommy LaSorda, the Hall of Fame Dodger manager, probably voiced best the difficulty in striking the right balance in leading a team. "Managing a team," LaSorda said, "is like holding a dove in your hands. Too tight, you squeeze it to death; too loose, it flies away." Only Casey Stengel may have expressed it even better: "The secret of managing," Old Case said, "is to keep the five guys who hate you away from the ten who haven't made up their minds."

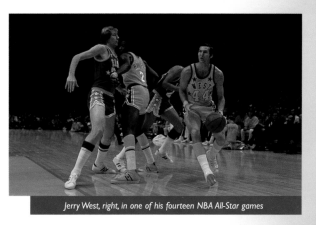

Jerry West, right, in one of his fourteen NBA All-Star games

But ultimately, teams win not only because individuals are prepared to subsume themselves into the group goal but because they learn to do it gracefully. It's not just a matter of doing the dirty work, blocking for the hotshot halfback, for instance; it's doing it without false humility. Good teams win because players revel in their roles, satisfied that, yes, sometimes they will get the chance to do what they do best, but in turn they must support their teammates when it is another's moment to shine.

Bill Russell, who led the Boston Celtics to ten championships in twelve years and who is generally regarded as the greatest team player of all time in any sport, likes to say that it was not rebounding or playing defense that made him such a team player. Rather, to best illustrate what team play truly is, he would cite a small ripple that was all but lost in the whole great river of a game.

After Russell caught a rebound and threw it out to start the fast break—say, to Bob Cousy—it was sometimes necessary to join the break himself, running frantically down one side of the court. In basketball this is called "filling the lane." Cousy was the middle lane, Russell the left, and, usually, Tommy Heinsohn the right. And Russell was sure that virtually every time Cousy would pass the ball to Heinsohn for the layup. But nevertheless, Russell says, even though he knew he would merely be running with no chance to get the ball, he had

U.S. goalie Brianna Scurry, left, punches the ball away

to do it and do it to the utmost of his speed and effort. Otherwise the defenders could match up with Cousy and Heinsohn and thwart the break. That is the essence of team effort, doing something not only altruistically but doing it unnoticed as well.

Ultimately, the word we commonly use in this context—*teamwork*—may not be the most accurate; more appropriate is *teamcare*. Working together as a team can never be realized until the players truly care, not only for one another as comrades but for the whole entity. Only then can a team expect to work to win. ★

SOCCER IN the rest of the world has always meant football played by men, but in the United States the sport has emerged with very much a feminine association. First, in the early 1990s, there were the "soccer moms" of political note. As the soccer moms went, so would go the country, it was said. And then at the end of the decade there was what David Letterman labeled "Babe City." It wasn't

U.S. women's soccer fans, Pasadena, California, July 10, 1999

much different, however. As the babes went, so, too, would go the country. And the country went wild. The U.S. Women's Soccer Team won all America's hearts.

It was the first time a women's team had ever achieved the kind of attention that, previously, only a few tennis players and figure skaters had received. "I'll tell you," a prescient Billie Jean King had said years ago when she was at the height of her powers, "It doesn't really matter how famous I am, or Chrissie Evert, or Peggy Fleming, whoever. Only when women have a popular team sport in this country can we begin to approach equity with men in sports."

The Women's Soccer Team sneaked up on glory, too. Even though the Americans won the

1999 WOMEN'S WORLD CUP
U.S. SOCCER TEAM

inaugural Women's World Cup in 1991 and made the semis in 1995, NBC didn't televise the network's own national team

as they won the gold medal at the United States' own Atlanta Olympics in 1996. Not till the summer of 1999, when the U.S. women began to pick up steam, did they acquire a real following.

They started by selling out Giants Stadium in New Jersey—79,000 to watch a victory over Denmark. Then came more packed houses in Chicago, Boston, Washington, the Bay Area. Delighted, worshipful young girls—their faces painted red, white, and blue—dragged their parents to the games. There were soccer dads now, too, all the more because David Letterman had certified the players as something more than players. "The U.S. team—this may come out wrong—I'll just say it now," Letterman sputtered. "Babe City, ladies and gentlemen, Babe City!"

Suddenly, just like Michael and Magic and Larry of a certain Dream Team past, the country was on a first-name basis with Mia and Julie and Michelle and Brandi and Kristie and Cindy. And there were even soccer moms on the soccer team. Joy Fawcett had two small children, Carla Overbeck, one.

By the time the United States faced off against China in the championship game on July 10 in Pasadena, women's soccer had moved from the agate type of the sports pages to headlines on page one. The Rose Bowl was jam-packed, ninety thousand strong—the largest

Brianna Scurry with a save in the World Cup championship game, Pasadena, California, July 10, 1999

crowd ever to watch women play sports, but perhaps more important, forty million Americans stayed inside on a lovely summer afternoon to watch the game on television. That was far and away the biggest American audience ever to watch the alien game of soccer. The team also hit a magazine grand slam, making the covers of *Sports Illustrated, Time, Newsweek,* and *People* all in one fell swoop. These women had become more than just Babe City; now they were America's Team and they had blended into a juggernaut.

The United States won, of course. Nobody will ever forget that, or the sight of Brandi Chastain waving her shirt after scoring the winning goal in a shoot-out after 120 minutes of scoreless play. The other American players descended on her in a happy heap, and the Rose Bowl rocked.

One of Chastain's teammates did not participate in that revelry. Michelle Akers, long a star on the U.S. team, was hooked up to an IV by then. A victim of chronic fatigue syndrome, Akers, thirty-three, playing in her swan song, had been felled by a collision late in regulation time and had to be taken off suffering from a concussion and dehydration. Fourteen years earlier she had been an original member of the women's national team and had scored the very first U.S. goal. Now, in the locker room, Akers heard the roar as Chastain's championship goal found the net and women's soccer found its place in the land. ★

Few moments are as indelibly etched in the American sports memory as Brandi Chastain's celebration after scoring the game-winning goal in the U.S. victory over China in the Women's World Cup championship game. It was the culmination of a team effort for a unique blend of upcoming stars and veteran pioneers of the sport in the United States

The American women celebrated not just a World Cup championship win over China in 1999. They capped off a dominating decade in international competition that began with their first World Cup title in 1991, a third place in 1995, an Olympic gold medal in 1996, and a silver medal in 2000. In the process the team became not just a national icon. They won the hearts and opened the eyes of a new generation of young female athletes.

Unlike most countries, the United States doesn't really care all that much about international sport. We save most of our emotions for our domestic teams. After all, as a nation we're bigger than just about everybody else, so we're almost always supposed to win. We didn't really root for the basketball Dream Team. No, we admired it as we would an art exhibit in a museum.

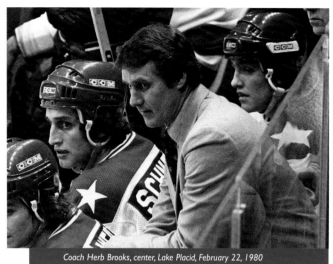

Coach Herb Brooks, center, Lake Placid, February 22, 1980

Of course, basketball is the prime American winter game, whereas ice hockey is a distinct fourth among our professional team sports. And amateur hockey? If, as 1980 began, you had asked even the most knowledgeable U.S. sports fans to name an amateur hockey player, hardly any could have ventured even a guess. To imagine then that a team of American nobodies, playing a generally unfamiliar sport in international play, could capture the affection of this disparate, distracted nation—well, that would be miraculous.

1980 U.S. OLYMPIC
HOCKEY TEAM

But it happened. The drama in Lake Placid was cast by events that took place far away and weeks before the Olympic Games began. In November, in Iran, sixty-three members of the American embassy were taken hostage, and as powerful as the United States might be, it was frustrated, a Gulliver pinned down by Lilliputians. Then, early in January, the Soviet Union attacked Afghanistan, and President Carter responded with economic sanctions and one symbolic action: He asked the U.S. Olympic Committee to keep the American hockey team from competing at the Moscow Games that summer. Tension between the two superpowers doubled.

While all this was happening, a forty-two-year-old college coach named Herb Brooks had been traveling with his first U. S. team, teaching his players a new, unfamiliar European style, forming a club that he thought might, with luck, win a bronze. Much of his coaching focused on motivation, the mind and the soul. He purposely kept his young charges off guard. At one point, after Brooks disparaged center Rob McLanahan, lacerating him as a "baby" and "a spoiled rich kid," McLanahan physically attacked his coach in the locker

★

"Do You Believe in Miracles?" became a mantra after the underdog U. S. Olympic hockey team stunned the world by winning the gold medal at Lake Placid, New York, in 1980. Goalie Jim Craig clutched both the flag and his goaltender's stick.

Team USA, Lake Placid, February 24, 1980

room. On another occasion, Brooks risked a team revolt by threatening to cut Mike Eruzione, the captain and senior man on the team (he was all of twenty-five). "It was basically us against the coach," remembers Steve Janazcak, the backup goalie. "I think this really brought the team together."

They cut it close, however. Only two weeks before the Olympics began, the Soviets toyed with Brooks's babies, clobbering them 10-3. The Soviet Union had won the last four Olympic golds. The champs were mature and seasoned, stocked with veteran players capable of being NHL stars had they not been barred from Western professionalism by their government.

But then, at Lake Placid, the Americans somehow came from behind to tie Sweden, then swept Czechoslovakia, Norway, Romania, and West Germany. American television viewers who didn't know a hockey puck from a badminton shuttlecock, had their heroes, and when the U.S. team faced off against the U.S.S.R. in the semifinals on February 22, it meant a whole new national experience. For once the United States was the underdog, the outmanned innocent. For Brooks and his players, it was kismet. "This moment is yours!" he cried out in the locker room. "You were meant to be here at this time." And sure enough, when Eruzione scored with ten minutes left, the U.S. team went ahead for good, 4-3.

Nevertheless, having beaten the big Russian bear, a letdown against Finland in the final was a distinct possibility, and sure enough the Finns led 2-1 after two periods. Then the U.S. team came alive, scored three more times, and by the end this team of strangers, assembled in obscurity and required to forget the way they had grown up playing hockey to learn a new style in just a few months—a style that required intricate passing and movement without the puck and a brand of teamwork none of them had experienced before—had become a whole nation's favorite sons. At the close of the century their triumph would be voted the American sports moment of the 1900s, and for the first Winter Games of the new millennium they would come together again to light the flame as a team. ★

The U. S. team adhered to the then-strict amateur rules governing Olympic hockey. This group of strangers struggled for months to learn the international style of hockey until they could play it with precision. By the time the Olympics had begun the Americans had bonded into a team with, as one Russian player put it later, "a spirit you could feel."

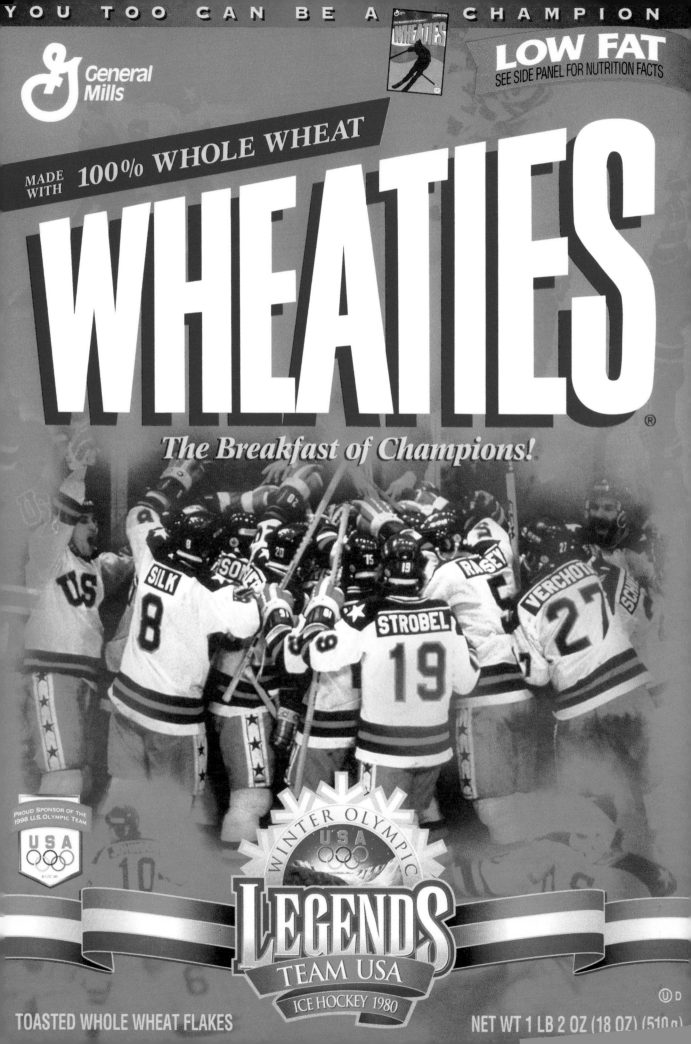

Generally speaking, Americans are divided between men and women, Democrats and Republicans, majority and minority, and Yankee lovers and Yankee haters. And glory be, it had been a joyously long epoch for the latter since 1978, when the arrogant pinstripe bullies had last won a World Series. Then, in the autumn of 1995, George Steinbrenner, the lord and master of the team, was presented with the possibility of hiring Joe Torre as the newest of his managers. This is an honor roughly akin to being selected as a bride of Henry VIII, but even then Steinbrenner was reluctant to tap Torre. "He's never won anywhere," the Boss snorted. In this regard he was right, too. Although Torre had spent thirty-two seasons in the majors as player and manager, he had never once been to a World Series. Even when Steinbrenner reluctantly agreed to hire Torre, others remained dubious. A New York tabloid headline greeted the choice, screaming, "CLUELESS JOE."

Joe Torre, left, and George Steinbrenner, Yankee Stadium, October 26, 1996

1996 WORLD SERIES CHAMPION
NEW YORK YANKEES

★

Yankee fans raised in the tradition of the Bronx Bombers, clubbing the opposition into submission were slow to warm to the World Champions of 1996, who won behind dependable pitching, brilliant defense, and such "small-ball" tactics as bunting runners into scoring position.

The following October, after Torre had led the Yankees to their first pennant in fifteen years, New York dropped the first two World Series games to Atlanta. Steinbrenner, still of little faith, said to his manager: "Let's not get embarrassed."

Torre replied calmly, "We'll be fine, George." And they were. The Yankees swept the next four games, and only then, as the whole team took a victory lap around Yankee Stadium (save for third baseman Wade Boggs, who hopped aboard a New York police department horse and circuited in the saddle), did Steinbrenner and the critics understand how special—and how different—was this twenty-third Yankee champion.

The Yankees had been playing in World Series since 1921 and winning them since 1923. But all previous Yankee champions had been distinguished by the fact that one or even two great

Mariano Duncan, center, and the Yankees, October 26, 1996

Hall of Fame sluggers anchored each team. Babe Ruth, of course, was the main attraction of the first cluster of Yankee titles. Lou Gehrig assisted the Bambino, then succeeded him as the bellwether of the 1930s champions, just as Joe DiMaggio became the centerpiece after Gehrig's death. As soon as DiMaggio retired, Mickey Mantle stepped forward. Then, after a while, Steinbrenner signed Reggie Jackson to play the leader's role.

Now, Torre's team was not without clout. Bernie Williams, a classical guitarist; Paul O'Neil, an unpredictable tempest; and Tino Martinez, who was brought in, impossibly, to replace the beloved Don Mattingly at first base—all three could deliver power. Moreover, rookie shortstop Derek Jeter—"the golden child of New York," Williams dubbed him—was obviously a star in the making. But Jeter was still only the juvenile lead. There was no Reggie to stir the drink, let alone a Sultan of Swat, an Iron Horse, a Yankee Clipper, or even just a Mick. For the first time the Bronx Bombers had to win without a prime Bomber.

If anything, pitching often had to carry the team. Significantly, it was the closer, John Wetteland, not any of the hitters, who was voted MVP of the 1996 Series. Andy Pettitte, only twenty-four, won twenty-one games to lead an eclectic starting staff that included the savvy David Cone, junkballer Jimmy Key, and Dwight Gooden, whom Steinbrenner rescued after drug rehabilitation (he would pitch a no-hitter in May). Perhaps most impressive was young Panamanian reliever Mariano Rivera, who somehow threw pitches at a hundred miles per hour even though he weighed in at only 168.

As it turned out, too, the 1996 team was only the start of a new juggernaut. But the key to the Yankees' success was no longer overwhelming power and talent as it once had been. This time around it was smart baseball by a group of team-oriented players who knew how to win games with situational hitting, sound defense, and steady pitching. They had become more an ensemble than a star vehicle. It was a confusing turnaround. Torre's Yankees were so proficient as a team on the field and so nice as individuals off it that they began to accomplish the unthinkable. Some Yankee haters actually began to love them. ★

★

After losing the first two games of the 1996 World Series to Atlanta, the Yankees won sixteen of the next seventeen games they played in baseball's ultimate event. That run resulted in four World Championships in a span of five seasons.

Jerry West: Sharpshooter from Cabin Creek

**by Bob Richards, Director
Wheaties Sports Federation**

He may not be as tall, as strong, or as fast as the other super stars of pro basketball, but no one has a deadlier shooting-eye than Jerry West, the backcourt star of the Los Angeles Lakers. He's won so many games with fantastic shooting in the closing seconds, that the other players call him Mr. Clutch.

In the mountain town of Cabin Creek, West Virginia where Jerry was raised, by the time you were 6 or 7 you learned to shoot — basketballs, that is. And Jerry learned his lesson well. To make up for his lack of size, he practiced his shooting day and night on a dirt court in his backyard.

"I practiced over and over — shooting the same shot from the same spot 'til I hit 10 in a row. Then I'd practice my moves to get to that spot over and over again."

As a 6'2", 150 lbs. high school forward, Jerry led his team to the state title his Senior year, then enrolled at the University of West Virginia. ("I'd seen them play when I was in high school, and I knew that's where I wanted to go.") Jerry's sharpshooting sparked the Mountaineers to 3 straight Southern Conference Titles.

In his Junior year he made the All-American team. Then, he proceeded to win the Most Valuable Player award in every post-season tournament he played in, including the NCAA where West Virginia lost in the finals despite a 29 point effort by Jerry. In his Senior year he again made the All-American team, and co-captained the U.S. Olympic basketball team.

Jerry's performance in the National Basketball Association has been no less amazing. In 7 seasons of hard work he has pushed his scoring average from 17 points per game to 30. He is consistently among the league leaders in scoring and assists, has made the All-Star team 6 straight years, and is the only backcourt man in the history of the sport to score over 60 points in one game. (He scored 63 against New York in 1962.)

"You never really stop West," said one coach, "you try any number of ways—play him close, loose, keep him away from the ball —and even then he'll get his 25 or 30 points a game."

In fact, the harder they try to stop him, the better Jerry gets — in the playoffs he scores more points, gets more assists and rebounds better than in a regular season game. "The harder things are, the better I like it," he says. "The challenge seems to lift me up."

How high is up? No one seems to know. As Laker general manager Fred Schaus puts it, "somehow, he just gets better year after year —and I think he'll keep on getting better, because he has desire." Back home in Cabin Creek, folks are quick to agree.

JERRY WEST WAS famous for losing, once in the finals of the NCAA championship with West Virginia and seven times in the NBA finals with the Lakers. His image was of a scorer, and, indeed, he averaged twenty-seven points a game, fourth best, all-time. He was the classic shooter who could do it all by himself: take the ball, move for the shot, give the ball one last high bounce—"come off the dribble" in basketball jargon—

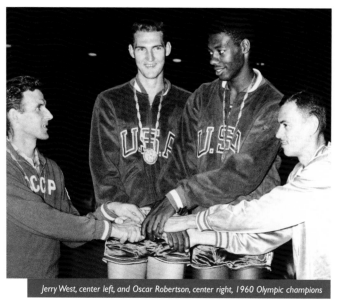

Jerry West, center left, and Oscar Robertson, center right, 1960 Olympic champions

quickly soaring, his thirty-eight-inch arms lifting the shot up and in. Why not? In his own yard in the hollows of West Virginia he had learned the game alone, concentrating on basketball, because, he would explain, "It is a game a boy can play by himself." West is even cast forever as the star alone, the model for the NBA logo.

MR. BASKETBALL
JERRY WEST

★

Jerry West was such an embodiment of individual grace as a player that the NBA chose his silhouette dribbling the ball as its logo. But his greater legacy may well be as the architect who designed two distinctly different Los Angeles Lakers championship dynasties in two different eras.

But in truth he was all the things integral to team. Because he scored so much, it eclipsed the fact that he was a peerless playmaker. He even led the league in assists one year. West was also a wonderfully instinctive defender, and probably no player at 6-feet-3 could rebound and block shots as well. Moreover, he was at his best under pressure—"Mr. Clutch," he was called. He had guts and grit. He broke his nose nine times; probably his most extraordinary effort came in 1969, in another one of those seventh games in the finals against the Celtics. West had pulled a hamstring and before the game had to be helped down the stairs to the court, a friend propping him up on either side. He scored forty-two points, grabbed thirteen rebounds, and passed for a dozen assists. And the Lakers lost again, by two. Even in their joy, the Celtics trooped in to console West. "I love you, Jerry," John Havlicek said. They all did, teammates and rivals. They knew every fiber of the man was dedicated to victory.

After another defeat by the Celtics, he drove his wife home after the game. At the house, he let her out and drove off to be by himself. It broke Jane West's heart, but she understood. "Jerry doesn't like anybody to see him cry," she said. He cried a lot. There were so many hard defeats before the victories finally came.

Jerry West's teams may not have won many championships during his playing career, but he played against the best, and the sight of his effort and poise has lingered in memory longer than the outcome of any particular game. Here he drove for a basket against Bill Russell and the Boston Celtics in the seventh game of the 1965 NBA finals, won by Boston.

JERRY WEST
guard

LOS ANGELES

★

Of Jerry West, legendary Los Angeles Lakers broadcaster Chick Hearn once said: "His number one concern was for the sport of basketball. Concern number two was for his team. And a distant third on his list was Jerry West."

West always remained exceptionally popular, for even as he was transformed from a shy and silent rustic—"Zeke from Cabin Creek"—into an outspoken and even garrulous presence, he never lost his basic, good-guy appeal. In 1971, when West was injured and on crutches, the Lakers feted him with a night. Bill Russell paid his own way to cross the country for the tribute. He hugged his old rival and said: "Jerry, the greatest honor a man can have is the respect and friendship of his peers. You have that more than any man I know. You are, in every sense of the word, a champion, and if I could have one wish granted, it would be that you would always be happy."

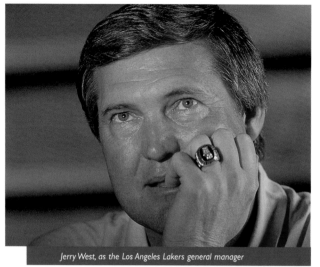

Jerry West, as the Los Angeles Lakers general manager

The next year West was healthy again and the Lakers won a record thirty-three games in a row, then took the only title West ever earned as a player. The championship had finally caught up with the champion.

Two years after injuries forced him to retire in 1974, Jerry West was named Los Angeles coach, although he only reluctantly accepted the position. He won one division title in his three years, but he was simply too high-strung to remain a coach. Even when he became general manager in 1982 he was often unable to watch the action, so he'd station himself by an exit where he could duck away in tense moments. Whereas few of the greatest players ever succeed in management, West became as superb a team builder as he had been a team leader. Under his guidance two distinct Laker conglomerates won titles, first in the 1980s, and then at the turn of the century before West retired after the 2000 season with this singular distinction: He had led his team as a player, he had led them as a coach, and he had built two world championship teams as general manager. ★

AMERICANS HAD A succession of love affairs with Olympic gymnasts that began in 1972 in Munich when ABC introduced a gymnastics-ignorant country to Olga Korbut. Four years later, Nadia Comaneci, with the sport's first perfect scores, stole the TV show that emanated from Montreal, and in 1984, at the Los Angeles Olympics that was boycotted by most of the Communist bloc, America's own Mary Lou Retton became our newest heroine.

But whereas gymnastics' level of participation in the United States soared thanks to its Olympic popularity, Retton's all-around triumph in Los Angeles remained an American aberration. In Seoul and then in Barcelona there were no new summer pixies to captivate us as Mary Lou had. Then in 1996 in Atlanta came a whole charming team—the Magnificent Seven (even if the seven themselves were too young to have known their original cinematic namesakes). All teenagers, they ranged from the old lady, nineteen-year-old captain, Amanda Borden, down to a fourteen-year-old, Dominique Moceanu. The U.S. squad was deep and versatile and close.

1996 WOMEN'S OLYMPIC
GYMNASTIC TEAM

★

Most Americans didn't even realize there was a team championship in Olympic gymnastics when the competition began in 1996 at Atlanta. By the end of the event a record number of televisions were tuned in to watch the injured Kerri Strug help vault the United States to the gold medal.

Gymnastics is one of those team sports that is essentially an individual game that only cumulatively builds up a total score. It is probably the most individualistic team sport. There are no relay races in gymnastics, no doubles or best ball matches. Maybe that makes it more difficult for the competitors: You are always performing alone, but the team depends utterly on your personal effort. There is nobody to pass the ball to, nobody to compensate for your mistakes.

Yet team chemistry matters in gymnastics as surely as it does in hockey or volleyball. The 1992 U.S. team members had been at odds, all the more so because the coaches wrangled shamelessly with one another. But in Atlanta the coaches were in synch, and the teammates close and supportive. Sequestered in a fraternity house at Emory University that was

From left, Amy Chow, Dominique Moceanu, and Amanda Borden, July 21, 1996

off-limits to the rest of the world, they had to get along. Captain Borden became a genuine team leader; not only did she rouse her troops but she sacrificed her own glory. Only six from a team compete in any event, with the five top scores counting, so she agreed to sit out the bars and vault competitions because she knew her teammates were stronger at those events. At the Georgia Dome the home-country crowd seemed to pick up on the team's spirit and echo it back to the American girls.

By gymnastics standards, at eighteen Kerri Strug was an old-timer. She had made the U. S. team at thirteen but had never quite lived up to her promise. "Scary Kerri," critics whispered of her in sarcastic tribute to her inconsistency. Even her coach, Bela Karolyi, referred to her insecurities. "Kerri has not a high tolerance for pain," Karolyi said. "She was never the toughest girl." By Atlanta, she was even playing second-fiddle in the Karolyi camp to Moceanu, the fourteen-year-old.

But Strug, like her teammates, performed solidly in the team competition, and the U.S. inched ahead of Russia. With Moceanu and Strug last to go on the vault, the Americans needed only one of the two to score 9.6 to ensure victory. But then Moceanu, unaccountably, fell on both her vaults, so winning depended entirely on Strug—all 4-feet-8 and (maybe) 90 pounds of her. And, on her first go, a one-and-a-half twisting Yurchkenko vault, she landed cleanly, but felt a crack. She had sprained her left ankle. In great pain and under the pressure only an Olympics can bring down on a performer, she had just thirty seconds before she had to vault again.

Somehow, Strug put the agony out of her mind. She prayed. She couldn't allow herself to limp, for that would have put her off her rhythm and destroyed any chance of a successful vault. She ran on the sprained ankle. She landed on it. Cleanly. Only then did she cry. Her score: 9.712. Gold. She wouldn't let them take her to the hospital until she could stand in victory with her gymnastic teammates. Her coach carried her to the podium, and Kerri Strug had one of the magnificent seven medals put round her neck. ★

The sense of "team" among the American women in the otherwise individual sport of gymnastics became clear as the final scores were being tabulated. The group assembled around coach Bela Karolyi, then erupted in unison to celebrate their dramatic victory.

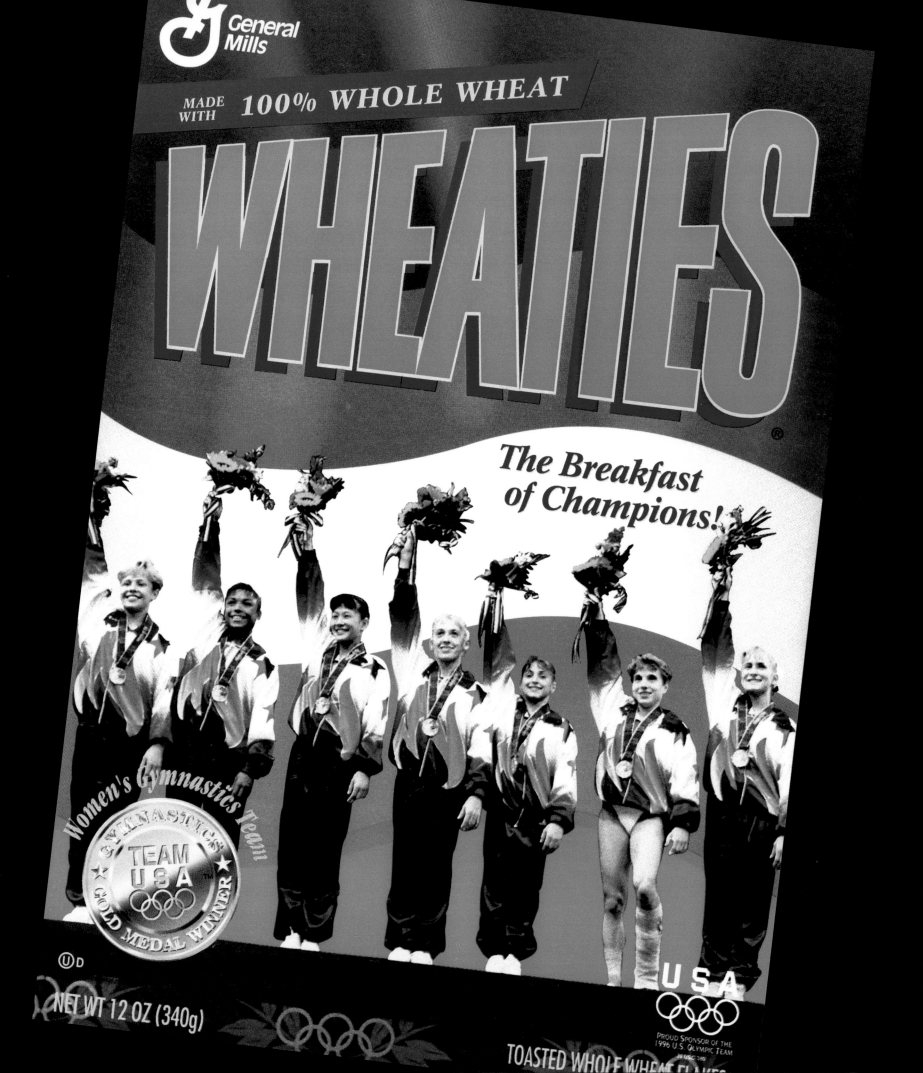

PERSEVERANCE

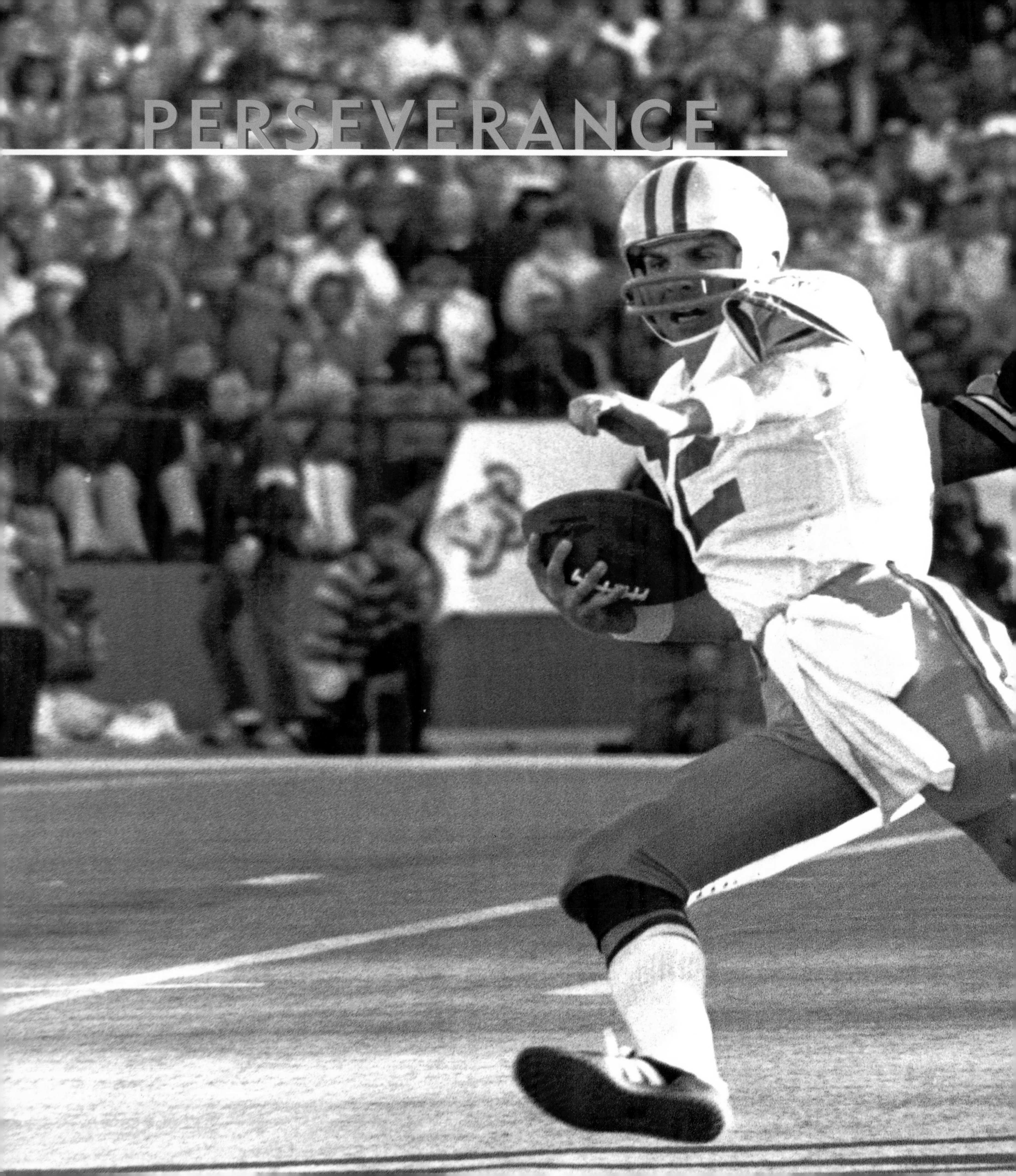

> *"Many of life's failures are people who did not realize how close they were to success when they gave up."* —THOMAS EDISON

PERSEVERANCE

As the late pitcher Catfish Hunter once remarked after a particularly tough loss, "The sun don't shine on the same dog every day." Athletes understand this intellectually, but emotionally it is the very capriciousness of sport that is often most difficult to accept. So often we hear someone say, "Hang in there; don't quit; never say die." All the glib locker-room entreaties from coaches who grew up studying Knute Rockne cry out for perseverance. Nor is it just a matter of fighting back from injury and bad luck.

Satchel Paige, Cleveland, July 7, 1948

No, the need to persevere confronts a player in much more subtle and complicated guises. Ironically, it is often the best athletes who have the most trouble accepting both the uncertainties of competition and the necessity of being hard-nosed and sticking with it. After all, virtually every athlete who reaches the highest levels of sport was a star at a lower level, and usually, too, the player who achieves early success is naturally blessed. Being good at that sport has come as a gift that often required little effort or self-searching. And then suddenly the young player reaches a point where everyone is at least pretty good, and God-given talents are no longer sufficient unto themselves. Many of the best athletes drop by the wayside relatively early, quitting because they are simply not prepared to work hard at what had previously been such a breeze.

I have always suspected that athletes who develop slowly physically will generally be a bit more stalwart than the more precocious achievers. Late bloomers have had to struggle early on; they become hardened to the struggle to improve, and when they finally do catch up with their peers, they often have more grit. Michael Jordan himself, cut from his high school team, is the classic of this type in the modern era. Big Bill Tilden, skinny and self-conscious, barely made his college team, but six years later he completely ruled tennis, acclaimed the greatest player ever to have picked up a racket.

Then, too, some athletes are done in by expectations. They are able to work their way up, but when they actually find themselves at the top, when they have achieved their dreams, the challenge of remaining there seems too daunting. "The toughest thing about success," Irving Berlin said, "is that you've got to keep on being a success." To persevere in victory is often more difficult than trying to rise up from defeat, although the latter of course is the model we invariably celebrate, the figure whom Hollywood, especially, adores. Think *Rocky, Hoosiers, The Bad News Bears*. Each so different, but the same story told over and over again. In fact, however, the champion who is able to steel himself or herself and remain a champion is in many respects the nobler character. Unfortunately, the tale of repeated success is neither so dramatic nor so touching, and so it is seldom prominent in our feel-good folklore. We prefer Cinderellas first and comebacks second. Often, in fact, the greatest of our sports heroes, those who dominate their game with apparent ease, do not engage

Billy Mills, left, Tokyo Summer Olympics, October 1964

us until they begin to decline. Then they are human. Then we finally allow ourselves to love them as Grand Old Men and Dear Old Women. Jack Nicklaus was such a figure. So was Chris Evert.

The finest competitors are those who are not afraid to lose—or, just as important, are not afraid to win. Who would be afraid to win, you may ask? More superb athletes than you can imagine. Of course everybody wants to win, but that's the very reason it can be so difficult and elusive for some. The ultimate in persevering is being able to close out the victory, to take over a game and end it your way. It is a quality often overlooked, but it is every bit as vital as fighting off defeat.

Bob Richards, Helsinki Summer Olympics, July 1952

And hooray for those who stay in the game without enjoying much success. There is a special place in sports heaven for them. Unfortunately, on the field of play it is rare for the ugly duckling to grow into a beautiful swan. Those who doggedly persist in any activity where success is unlikely are the sportsmen and sportswomen we should most admire. Sports journalists learn early on that they are more likely to find the nicest and smartest types down at the end of the bench. And there is a greater, more tangible reward in that perseverance, too. Those are the ones most likely to become coaches, the ones who stay in the game and influence it the most, long after the best players have lost their physical gifts and have gone on to other lives. ★

WHEREAS A HANDFUL of women athletes had attained fame earlier in the twentieth century—Suzanne Lenglen and Helen Wills in tennis, Sonja Henie in figure skating, Gertrude Ederle for swimming the English Channel—Mildred Didrikson, the Texas daughter of Norwegian immigrants, arrived as a force of female nature that had never been imagined before. It is even fair to say that she excelled in more diverse sports than any person in history. And like that unique character George Herman Ruth, from whom she drew her nickname, she was an original creation who was adored by some and disdained by others but who was always the center of fascination. "Well," she would say, entering the locker room, "Babe's here now. Who's gonna come in second?"

Babe Didrikson, New Orleans, March 27, 1934

Like Babe Ruth, too, whose greatness and charisma restored faith in baseball after the Black Sox scandal, Babe Didrikson's extraordinary performance at the 1932 Olympics had much to do with saving the honor of women's sport. In 1928 Babe, a high school dropout, had been working as a stenographer in Dallas when women's track and field had finally been

THE GREATEST ATHLETE
"BABE" DIDRIKSON

allowed into the Olympics. After a hard-raced 800 meters, however, a couple of the competitors collapsed from exhaustion and the hand-wringing suddenly began. Overwrought, overprotective men rushed to save these dear, dainty competitors from their exertions, banning all races longer than 100 meters. The fear that sport was bad for women, that training damaged their reproductive capacity, was widespread. Maybe it would be best to restrict women's competition to the more genteel activities, like croquet.

And then came Babe from out of nowhere—"the ultimate Amazon, the greatest athlete of all mankind for all time," the era's premier sportswriter, Grantland Rice, hailed her. Already a basketball star who routinely scored thirty points a game at a time when most teams failed to reach twenty, Didrikson had also hit .400 in softball, starred in volleyball, had mastered bowling, tennis, and diving, and had become, literally, a one-woman track

★

Babe longed to compete as an equal with men. She struck out Joe DiMaggio in an exhibition game and scrimmaged with the SMU football team. But she withdrew from a boxing match, saying, "I've decided I want to be a lady."

Babe Didrikson, right, and Jimmy Foxx, March 20, 1934

team. At the U.S. Olympic tryouts she entered eight of the ten events, won five, and tied for first in another, totaling thirty points. Runner-up was the Illinois Women's Athletic Club, which, with twenty members, amassed twenty-two points.

Fearful that such a fragile vessel must be restrained, Didrikson was allowed to compete in only three events at the Games in Los Angeles. She set records to win the 80-meter hurdles and the javelin and tied for first in the high jump. Notwithstanding, Didrikson was criticized in some circles for her unladylike coarseness and for her mannish appearance. She was also criticized for her disdain for her supposed "place" as a woman in America. One New Yorker wrote, "It would be much better if she and her ilk stayed at home, got themselves prettied up, and waited for the phone to ring." Needless to say, Babe endured.

By the mid-1940s she had begun to concentrate on golf, soon becoming the best woman golfer in the world. As an amateur she won seventeen tournaments in a row. As a pro she won the U.S. Open in 1948 and 1950, sweeping what counted then as the Triple Crown of women's golf in the latter year and topping the money-winning list from 1948 through 1951. No woman could approach her drives off the tee. "You've just got to loosen your girdle and really let the ball have it," she explained to a press that had come to adore her. So, more and more, did the fans. She even wowed them on stage, blowing a mean harmonica on *The Ed Sullivan Show*.

And then, when only thirty-eight, Didrikson was diagnosed with colon cancer. Operated on in the spring of 1953, she was, incredibly, back playing before the summer was out; she actually won a tournament six months after major surgery. Didrikson took her third U.S. Open the next year and, perhaps more amazing, posted the lowest average score for the year. Only her close friends knew, however, that her cancer had returned. In pain, unable to put on spikes, Babe Didrikson won her last LPGA tournament in 1955 wearing loafers.

When she died the next September 26 at the age of forty-two, President Dwight D. Eisenhower delayed a scheduled press conference to pay tribute to this greatest of American athletes, she whose talent, at the end, was only exceeded by her nobility. ★

★

After winning Olympic gold medals in track and competing in everything from tennis to bowling, baseball to football, and skating to shooting, Babe took up golf because it was the only sport left open to her. Able to drive farther than most men, she helped launch the women's pro tour and won three U.S. Women's Open titles.

A star in every sport she took up, Babe was not only unafraid to fail, she rarely did, even while constantly seeking new challenges. Here, second from right, she won the gold medal in the women's 80-meter hurdles at the 1932 Olympics in Los Angeles. She set a world and Olympic record of 11.7 seconds in this race.

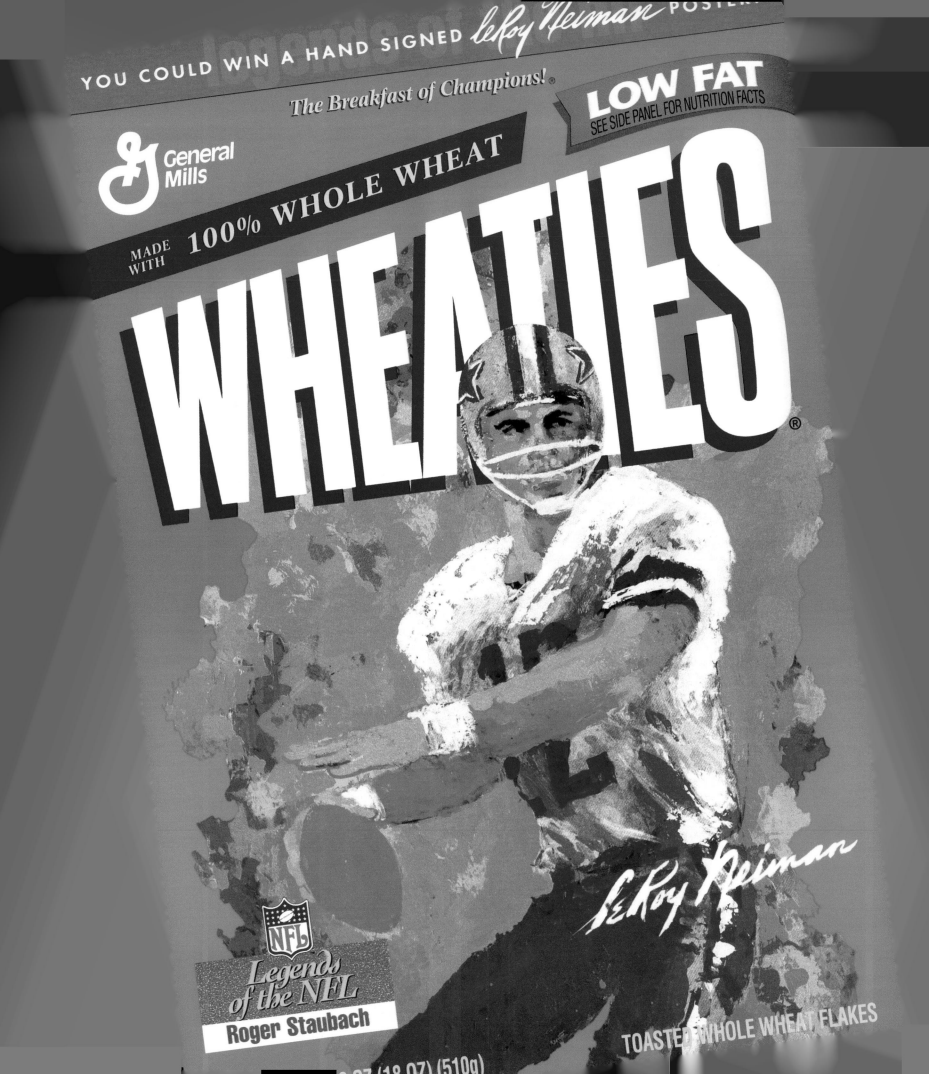

FOR SOMEONE SO disciplined and organized, there is an irony to Roger Staubach's career: It was always a little out of joint. Unlike most celebrated football prospects, he chose to attend a service academy, a commitment he knew would forestall any professional football opportunity. He was the last of the great football players to make that choice, a twenty-seven-year-old NFL rookie who would become a first-ballot Hall of Famer

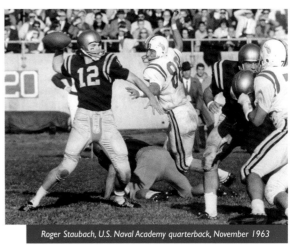

Roger Staubach, U.S. Naval Academy quarterback, November 1963

almost exclusively for what he accomplished after he turned thirty. And perhaps most interesting of all, because Staubach was so clean-cut and because he and his coach, Tom Landry, were such deeply religious, dependable types, they were the flip side to the glittery Cowboy Cheerleaders, thus providing that neat combination of contrasts that made Dallas "America's Team."

Among history's best quarterbacks, Staubach is the one invariably characterized first for his ability to inspire and command. Although he was hardly a romantic figure in the style of Unitas or Montana, Staubach was known as "Captain Comeback." Twenty-three times he

ROGER THE DODGER
ROGER STAUBACH

led the Cowboys back to victory from fourth-quarter deficits; more remarkable, on fourteen of those occasions he pulled it off

★

Staubach, a two-time All-American, and Heisman Trophy winner as a junior, appeared on the cover of Life magazine, right, on November 29, 1963. Dedicated to his ideals, he served out his military commitment, including a year in Vietnam, before entering the NFL.

with less than two minutes remaining or in overtime. "Roger never knew when the game was over," said one of his tight ends, Billy Joe DuPree.

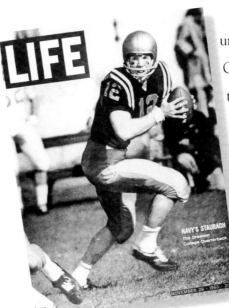

When Staubach chose to attend the Naval Academy, he understood very well the athletic implications of that decision. Other outstanding athletes had chosen military school, but of the four previous Heisman Trophy winners from West Point and Annapolis—Doc Blanchard, Glenn Davis, Pete Dawkins, and Joe Bellino—only Davis would enjoy even a modestly successful NFL career. By the time Staubach entered college, great athletes were at no risk in the military draft, either. They could join the reserves, serve six months on active duty during one off-season, and never have their pro careers affected. So, even though he had won the Heisman and been the most glamorously publicized of All-Americans at Navy, even though he would be among only eighty-three players chosen on the Walter Camp All-Century College Team, Staubach's five-year military commitment turned the pros off. The Cowboys made him a throwaway draft pick in the tenth round.

Roger Staubach, 12, Dallas cowboys quarterback, vs. Miami Dolphins

Staubach exhibited a patience the NFL scouts didn't have, however. During all his service time he studied the Cowboys' playbooks and, save for the year he was on duty in Vietnam, he arranged his leave so that he might attend the team's training camps. He was rusty when he finally mustered out of the navy, and it was another two seasons before Landry would start him, in mid-season, but when the chance came, Staubach was ready. He promptly won the league's quarterback title and, as the Super Bowl MVP, took Dallas to its first championship.

Essentially, the Staubach era was the seventies. Six times in that decade the Cowboys played in the National Conference title game. Four times they made the Super Bowl; twice they won. It is instructive that even though he retired as the highest-ranked passer in history, he was never voted to an All-Pro team. Rather, Staubach was one of those players who was greater than the sum of his statistics. Apart from passing for almost 23,000 yards, "Roger the Dodger" ran for more than 2,000 yards, and, even more important, the incalculable inspirational qualities he possessed allowed him to, on occasion, carry the whole team .

On retirement after the 1979 season, leaving at the top of his game, after yet another season as the league's best passer, Staubach shifted comfortably into business. Just as he had carefully prepared for pro football while in the Navy, he had become involved in real estate after moving to Dallas, and The Staubach Company, with twelve hundred employees, was soon a successful commercial real estate enterprise in North Texas. He has also been prominently associated with many good works and has been saluted by civic, business, religious, and charitable organizations, as well as by his alma mater, where he was chosen for the Naval Academy's Most Distinguished Graduate Award.

Someone once asked Staubach how he liked to be remembered in football. "As a pretty darn consistent quarterback," he said. But then, he has led a pretty darn consistent life in all its facets. ★

★

Although he didn't make his debut with the Cowboys until the age of twenty-seven, Roger Staubach led the NFL in passing four times and was a dangerous scrambler who always seemed to find an escape from the arms of would-be tacklers. His agility and his ability to make decisions on the fly made him a deadly comeback quarterback.

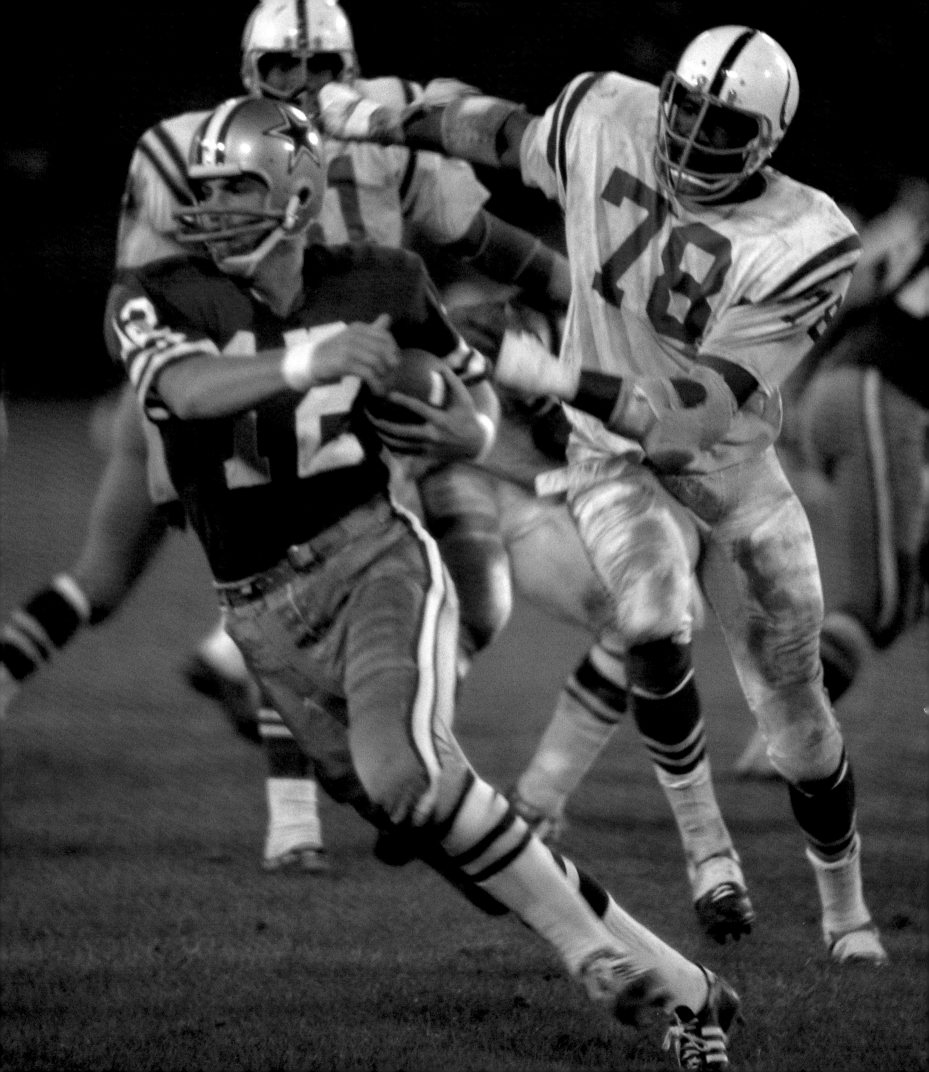

WAS ANY ATHLETE ever so indomitable as Satchel Paige? The sixth of twelve children, he was born in poverty in Alabama in 1906 and was working as a porter at the Mobile train station when he was only seven. There, for his ability to tote suitcases, Leroy became Satchel. However, the youngster who was sent to work in his childhood, whose family was too poor to afford toys, was caught stealing toys and, at age twelve began five-and-a-half years in the Industrial School for Negro Children. There he learned baseball and on release in 1924 began his long diamond odyssey.

Barnstorming through the backwaters of America's segregated Negro Leagues, with side trips to the Caribbean and Central and South America, Paige developed a reputation as perhaps the fastest and greatest pitcher in history. The best estimates are that he probably started 2,500 games and won 2,000 of them, with 250 shutouts, and 40 no-hitters, and tens of thousands of strikeouts. Sometimes he started as many as two hundred games in a single year yet, through all this, he kept his right arm alive. Somewhere the seemingly ageless man-child developed his Six Rules of Longevity.

ETERNAL YOUTH
SATCHEL PAIGE

★

A star in the Negro Leagues before World War II, Satchel Paige beat Dizzy Dean, right, and Bob Feller and struck out the likes of Joe DiMaggio, Hack Wilson, and Rogers Hornsby in exhibitions. He longed to be the first Black in the major leagues, but the honor went to a younger Jackie Robinson.

1.) *Avoid fried meats which angry-up the blood.*

But never mind the sketchy statistics. The white major leaguers he faced in autumn exhibitions spread the more vivid tales of his exploits. "The best I've faced and the fastest," Joe DiMaggio would say. Once Paige struck out twenty-two big leaguers in a single game. In a series he beat Dizzy Dean four games to two. "My fastball looks like a change of pace alongside that pistol bullet old Satch shoots up to the plate," Diz exclaimed. But then Paige calmly confounded hitters with his exquisite control as much as with the sheer speed he unleashed from his 180-pound, 6-feet-3 body.

Satchel Paige, tall man in hat, with some of his fans, 1941

2.) *If your stomach disputes you, lie down and pacify it with cool thoughts.*

Locked out of the majors because of his race, Paige would play anywhere for a price. Once he pitched in the Dominican Republic for the dictator Rafael Trujillo's team in a series that was supposed to determine an election. Spectators came packing guns, so Paige arranged with the local constabulary to escort him off the island as soon as was over. Then he coolly pitched his team to victory. Old Satch was always a show. Sometimes he ordered the outfield in while he struck out a batter or two. Against lesser local teams, he would blithely live up to his promise to strike out the first nine batters.

3.) *Keep the juices flowing by jangling around gently as you move.*

In 1938, pitching in the Mexican League, Paige finally came down with arm trouble, so he developed breaking balls and his fabled "hesitation pitch," leading the Kansas City Monarchs to five pennants in nine years. It was the last hurrah for the Negro Leagues however, because in 1946 the Brooklyn Dodgers signed Paige's teammate, Jackie Robinson, to a contract. Paige had always dreamed of being the first African-American in the majors, but when integration finally came, he was past forty and it was the younger Black players the majors were scouting.

4.) *Go very light on the vices, such as carrying on in society. The societal ramble ain't restful.*

Then, on his forty-second birthday, July 7, 1948, Bill Veeck, the owner of the Cleveland Indians, signed Paige, giving him a rocking chair in the bullpen. *The Sporting News,* the self-proclaimed "Bible of Baseball," called the signing demeaning—and never mind, as Veeck pointed out, that this was only justice delayed by a quarter-century. As for the resolute Paige, he went 6-1, with two shutouts and a 2.48 ERA; for one game he started, he drew a record crowd of 78,382.

5.) *Avoid running at all times.*

Old Satch finally began to wear down, but as late as 1965 the Kansas City Athletics hired him to work a game, and, at the age of fifty-nine, the oldest major-league pitcher ever, he threw three innings against the Boston Red Sox, allowing just one hit.

6.) *Don't look back. Something might be gaining on you.*

Long overdue, fame, honor, and respect had finally caught up with him. In 1971, when the Baseball Hall of Fame was opened to Negro League players, only one man was honored that first year—Satchel Paige. ★

★

Legendary Cool Papa Bell said, "Some people say that I was born too soon, but that's not true—they opened the doors too late." With those words, Baseball Hall of Famer Cool Papa Bell summed up the fate of most Negro League players. Paige described Bell as being so fast he could flip off the light and get into bed before the light went out (Cool Papa was clocked circling the bases in 11 seconds). Paige's perseverance did finally pay off, even if his fastball no longer had what former teammate Josh Gibson had called "a snap at the end that made it disappear."

AN OGALA SIOUX INDIAN, Billy Mills has always thought of himself as a warrior. Crazy Horse is his hero. It disturbs him greatly that the name of the great chief is now identified mostly with brand names and with a dance hall in Paris. "People would rise up in arms if there was a beer named 'Martin Luther King Malt Liquor,'" he says indignantly when he speaks to the young Native American children whom he lectures to and mentors.

Billy Mills, No. 722, Tokyo, October 1964

Mills tells his listeners that in the modern world a warrior is not simply someone who goes to battle. In the more than eighty countries he has visited, Mills has met thousands of athletes, and he sees in them a warrior sensitivity that still motivates him in his sixties.

"A warrior leads his or her life in four areas," Mills says. "Number one, the warrior assumes self-responsibility.

"And as the warrior becomes responsible for himself or others, the warrior never forgets

THE WARRIOR'S WAY
BILLY MILLS

★

Billy Mills started running shortly after being orphaned at the age of twelve. Fifteen years and, by his estimate, 45,000 miles later, he stunned the world by becoming the only American to ever win the Olympic gold medal in the 10,000-meter run.

humility. We are no better—or no worse—than another. So as the warrior assumes self-responsibility, then the warrior reaches out and helps other people become responsible.

"The third thing the warrior learns is the power of giving. You learn to give respect for yourself, so you will respect one another.

"And a warrior takes responsibility, humility, and the power of giving and centers that around his or her core of spirituality."

Certainly it is unusual to identify warring with those benign attributes of responsibility, humility, generosity, and spirituality, but then neither would one be likely to imagine that an impoverished orphan child named Loves His Country would become an Olympic champion. So implausible is the Billy Mills story, so unexpected was his great triumph in 1964, that as he still fought for breath after crossing the finish line, the first question a sports journalist asked him was, "Who are you?"

Mills was twenty-six that summer, a first lieutenant in the Marine Corps who had given up running but had gone back into training in the wistful hope of

Billy Mills, Tokyo, October 1964

qualifying for the games. Nothing unusual for him in that. Mills had always tended to come in by the side door. He had started running only as roadwork, a way of building up stamina in his training to become a boxer.

Born in Pine Ridge, South Dakota, soon to be a child alone without mother or father, Mills was admitted to the Haskell Institute, a school for young Native Americans in Lawrence, Kansas. It was there that he flourished as a runner, earning an athletic scholarship to the University of Kansas. Mills became an All-American in cross-country, achieving a more modest degree of success in the two-mile. Really, on KU's national championship track team Mills was hardly more than a face in the crowd, and by the time he qualified for the U.S. team and reached Tokyo, it was another Kansas runner, a miler still in high school named Jim Ryun, who was attracting the lion's share of the attention.

Mills was competing in the 10,000 meters, a race that Americans had rarely seriously contested. Not only that, Ron Clarke of Australia, the world-record holder, was a strong favorite. In the preliminary heats, Mills ran only a 29:10, almost a full minute slower than Clarke.

So even as Mills stayed up near the leaders as the long race wore on, he was strictly another *who-are-you*. Moreover, his quixotic challenge was all but ruined when, on the penultimate lap, he found himself behind a pack of tiring runners. Mills had to come around the outside, but he caught up with Clarke and Mohammed Gammoudi of Tunisia and then somehow, down the stretch, found some source of energy deep within himself and sprinted past the leaders to victory. He had run the last lap in 59.8 seconds, and, more incredibly, his time for the 10,000 was 28:24. Runners usually improve only by tiny increments, even by split seconds. In his most important race, faced with running a longer distance because he had to pass on the outside, Billy Mills had run almost a whole minute better than he had ever run before.

In the moment he came to the final turn, challenged by a chance for glory, Billy Mills—Loves His Country—heard an inner voice asking, "Who are you?" By the time he crossed the finish line and heard the question again from that reporter, the humble warrior knew. Even now, no other American has ever won gold in the 10,000 meters. ★

★

Billy Mills's 10,000-meter victory at Tokyo in 1964 is considered one of the greatest upsets in Olympics history. Australian Ron Clarke was heavily favored. And Mills's record time of 28 minutes, 24.4 seconds was his personal best by 45 seconds.

Bob Richards:
"The Sky's the Limit"

He's a two-time Olympic pole vaulting champion, three-time U. S. Decathlon champion, a member of the Helms Sports Hall of Fame, and a Minister-At-Large for the Church of the Brethren.

Sound like a fictional hero? Maybe. But in this case, it happens to be true. The man is Bob Richards, one of the greatest champions of our time.

In high school, he was a three-letter man. But his first love was pole vaulting. With a crossbar hooked between a tree and a telephone pole, he practiced hour on end in the back of his yard.

"I kept a picture of Cornelius Warmerdam clearing fifteen feet taped to the wall in my room," he says. His dream: to become the second man in history to clear that height (remember this was before the advent of the fiberglas pole).

In junior college, his best jump was 12'6". But at the University of Illinois there were guys who could clear that in their sweat suits. Did it discourage Bob?

"I began to lift weights as I had never lifted before. I began to sprint. I climbed rope. I did everything I

could to build myself up."

That same year he tied for first place in the Chicago Relays. And two years later he cleared the bar at 14 feet to tie for the National Collegiate Track Championship.

The following year he won the AAU title with a jump of 14'6", and placed third in the Olympics.

Then, in the 1951 Millrose Games he fulfilled his dream—becoming the second man in history to clear fifteen feet. "It was the greatest thrill of my life," he says, "I'd spent thousands of hours working for it."

Next, Bob began training for the Decathlon—ten grueling events rolled into one. ("This guy challenged me to do it," he says simply.) Within four months he had won the AAU title setting a new record.

Bob won the national decathlon championship again in 1954 and '55. But his greatest triumphs came in pole vaulting.

In the 1952 Olympic Games he won a gold medal with a record-breaking jump of 14'11". And in 1956, he repeated the feat becoming the only man in history to win two Olympic gold medals in the event.

Yet, Bob's story does not end there. Today as Minister-At-Large for the Church of the Brethren, and head of the Wheaties Sports Federation, he travels around the country giving inspirational talks to interested groups. His subject? ". . . There's no limit to what a man can do. If he believes in himself, if he works hard—the sky's the limit."

OF THE NEARLY two hundred athletes and forty-seven teams that have appeared on Wheaties boxes, none was ever so identified with the product as Bob Richards. All athletes already enjoy a certain certification when they are chosen to adorn a Wheaties box, and so it was with Richards when his image first appeared on the box in 1958. But his close and very visible association with the cereal would last for another half-century and so, especially since he came from a relatively obscure sport, only Bob Richards ultimately became more famous for being on the box than for getting on the box.

While that is quite a testament to his personality and persuasive charm, it's also not very fair to Richards's athletic prowess. He had dominated his sport for as long as he later ruled the cereal world. Richards is still the only man to have won two Olympic gold medals in the pole vault—in 1952 and 1956—and he had also won a third medal, a bronze, in 1948.

The heights he achieved fifty years ago seem humdrum inasmuch as today's vaulters approach twenty feet, but perhaps no sport has been so affected by technology as the pole vault. Richards and his contemporaries used wood poles. He would chug down the runway, plant the pole, and muscle himself up and over the bar. The word often used to describe his action was "jackknife." All this changed shortly after Richards's retirement when synthetic materials like fiberglass came into use. Thereafter vaulters could use their weight to bend their poles so as to slingshot themselves over the bar.

VAULT TO THE TOP
BOB RICHARDS

How good was Richards at his old-fashioned task? Well, even in track and field events dominated by one standout, the next best competitors are invariably only split seconds or centimeters behind. But until late in his career Richards was one of only two men ever to have topped fifteen feet. The first to achieve this, Cornelius Warmerdam, managed it on forty-three occasions between 1940 and 1944. Richards reached the fifteen-foot mark in 1951 and then did it 128 more times. Richards won the pole vault at New York's Millrose Games ten years in a row, a standard for sustained excellence that may not be matched anywhere in sport.

Bob Richards, left, with fellow U.S. pole vaulters Don Laz and George Mattos at the Helsinki Olympics in 1952, took great pride in being both a man of the cloth and a great athlete. He was known throughout the track world as the Reverend Bob Richards.

★

The dynamics of the pole vault were much different fifty years ago. Whereas today's fiberglass poles sling the vaulter over the bar, the wood poles of Richards's era had little flex. At the top of the vault, the athlete would literally do a pull-up from the pole to clear the bar, a feat that demanded considerable arm and upper-body strength.

Besides, he was too short to do what he did. Warmerdam, for example, was almost three inches taller than Richards. Don Bragg, who succeeded Richards as Olympic champion, was almost a half-foot taller. Just under 5-feet-10, Richards was limited in how high up he could hold his pole. When he was at the University of Illinois a physics professor proved absolutely that he could not possibly go more than fourteen feet, two inches. Bob Richards willed himself another foot and more.

Bob Richards explains pole vaulting technique, June 1958

Said Payton Jordan, a distinguished American track coach at that time: "Bob has the indomitable spirit to win and a firm belief that he can do better than he is supposed to. His stature limits his potential, but there is no limit on his determination." Indeed, once Richards had mastered the vault he took up other disciplines and three times triumphed as U.S. decathlon champion.

Richards's indefatigable nature had been evident early on. When he was an infant in Illinois, his baby buggy broke free into the street, where it was run over by a Model-T. He recovered, no worse for wear, and as he grew up he sought to become a boxer. Then, turning the other cheek, he gave up the square ring for the high bar while also studying for the ministry. He was ordained as a preacher when he was only twenty-two. Sportswriters, who were addicted to nicknames then, could not help dubbing Richards the "Vaulting Vicar." His was such an appealing story that a movie, *Leap to Heaven,* was made with Richards playing himself. He got pretty good acting notices, too.

The Rev. Mr. Richards became a prominent secular evangelist as well, preaching the gospel of physical fitness. "I want to urge every American to get off his duff," he stoutly declared. As for himself, every day he did pull-ups and push-ups, lifted weights, trampolined, and rode a bike. And, as everybody knew, he ate his Wheaties religiously. ★

★

Bob Richards showed his technique, left, at a Junior Champ Day sponsored by Wheaties. He used his fame and his glowing personality to encourage youngsters to take up sport and to eat right and become physically fit long before fitness became a pastime.

DREAMS OF GLORY

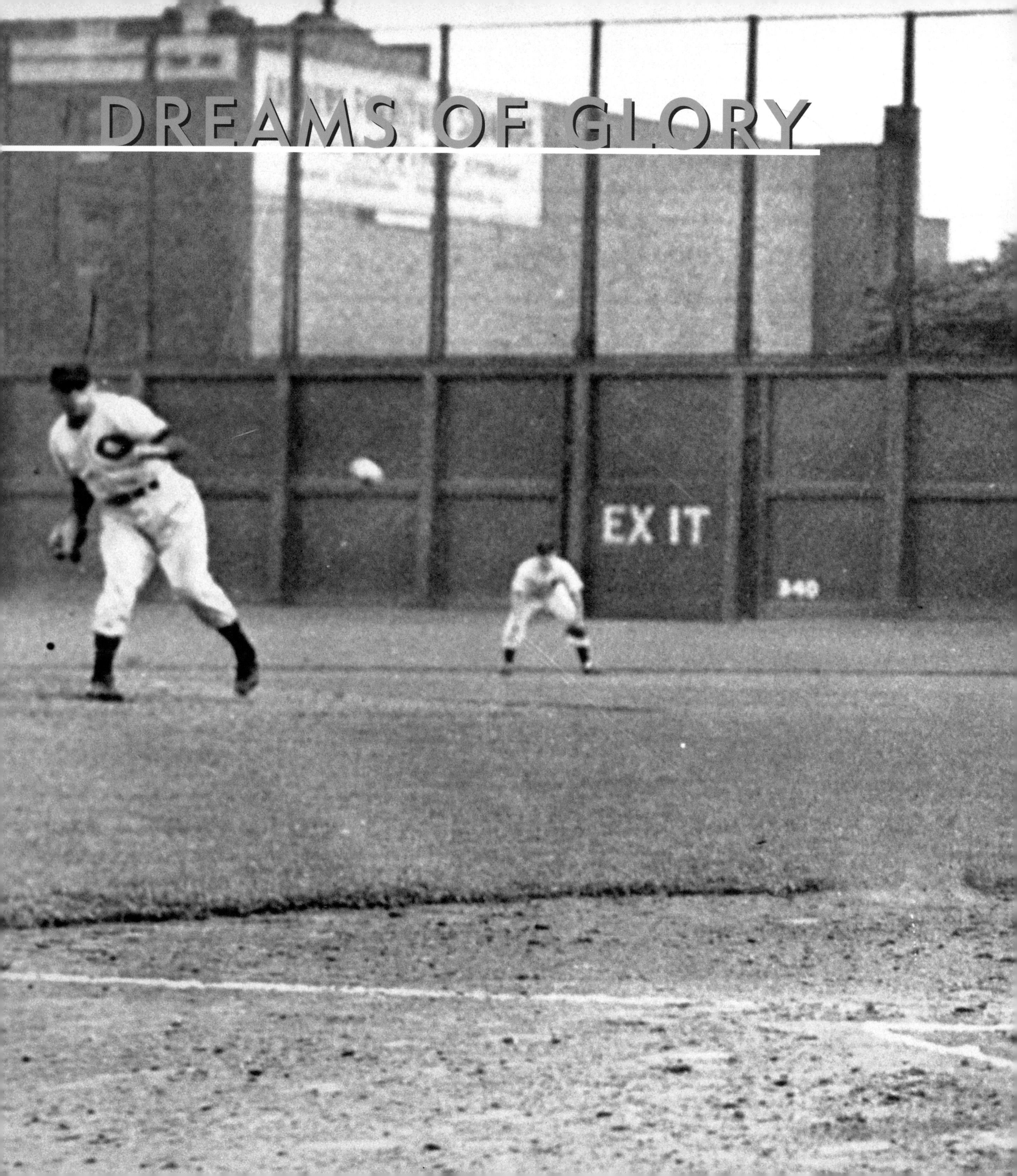

Bobby Jones
wins the 1923 U.S.
Open on the final hole
of an eighteen-hole
playoff. This win was
the first of his thirteen
major championships.

DREAMS OF GLORY

1923, 1924

IN THE EARLY YEARS of the twentieth century, sports were an outdoor pastime. Events were held in stadiums where fans—mostly men—went to see the game. Sometime after 1920 it all began to change. It might have begun when Babe Ruth became a Yankee and began to establish himself as a cultural icon. In August 1921, the first radio broadcast of a baseball game was done, and that October, a World Series game first came into America's living rooms. By the end of the decade, radio was regularly carrying baseball and football from the stadium to the home. What's more, the sports event itself had become transformed. It had become something more than a spectacle in a stadium—now it took place in the imagination of the listener. The heroes of the game had truly entered our consciousness.

Athletes had been held up to public view as role models. Baseball shortstop Honus Wagner was well aware of this nearly a century ago when he refused to grant a tobacco company permission to put his image on a card and made them stop the presses. Legend says Wagner used tobacco himself, but didn't want kids to be influenced to use it. Whatever the reason, his refusal made the surviving few Wagner cards worth many times more today than he ever earned as a player in his Hall of Fame career. Wagner was not only a role model, he has become an icon in spite of the rarity of his images.

★

Babe Ruth
becomes a Yankee on
January 3, 1920, when
he is sold to New York
by the Boston Red
Sox. Ruth went from
being a star pitcher to
a home run hitter and
revolutionized baseball.

Rogers Hornsby,
St. Louis Cardinals shortstop, finishes the regular
season with a .424 batting
average, the highest single
season batting average
of the century, September
30, 1924.

(continued on page 168)

Babe Ruth

hits his sixtieth home run of the season, September 30, 1927, breaking his previous record of fifty-nine. The record would stand for thirty-four years.

Ty Cobb

gets the 4,000th hit of his career, July 18, 1927. He went on to amass 4,191 hits.

WHOLE WHEAT FLAKES

WHEATIES

WITH ALL THE BRAN

SOLD MEDAL FLOUR

1925, 1926, 1927, 1928, 1929

National Football League

has a new rival, the American Football League, founded in 1926. The AFL lasts one year, and its remaining teams are absorbed into the NFL in 1927.

Helen Wills Moody

wins the first of her eight Wimbledon championships, 1927.

Red Grange

runs for four touchdowns and 262 yards on his first four carries to lead Illinois past Michigan 39-14, October 18, 1924.

WALTER JOHNSON
The famous Pitcher of the Washington American team, says:

Tuxedo is the one tobacco that contains every desired element. It is the best tobacco I have ever smoked." *Walter Johnson*

Tuxedo
The Perfect Tobacco
For Pipe and Cigarette

Jack Dempsey,

former heavyweight champion, loses the "Battle of the Long Count," when he fails to go to a neutral corner, giving champion Gene Tunney more time to get to his feet after a knockdown.

Denotes athletes appearing on Wheaties boxes ★

Statistical resources are Associated Press, Sports CNNSI, and personal biographies

John Wooden
earns all-American honors in 1930–31–32 at Purdue, and is named College Player of the Year in 1932.

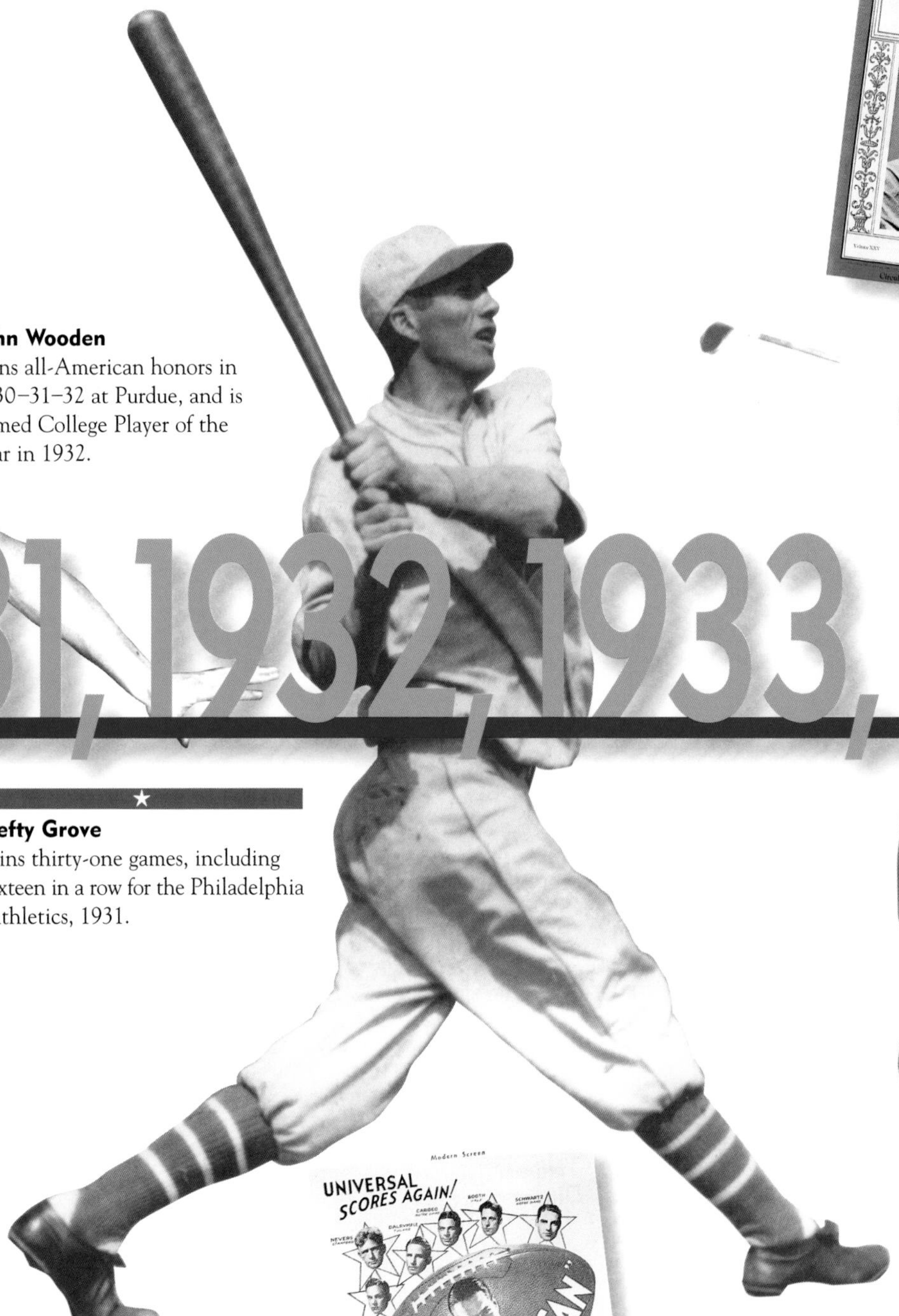

1930, 1931, 1932, 1933, 1934

★

Lefty Grove
wins thirty-one games, including sixteen in a row for the Philadelphia Athletics, 1931.

UNIVERSAL
SCORES AGAIN!

Modern Screen

"THE
ALL AMERICAN"
Universal Pictures

Glenna Collett Vare,
the "female Bobby Jones," wins her record sixth U.S. Womens' Amateur title in 1935. Known for her 300-yard drives, she played in tournaments until she was seventy.

Jesse Owens,
who a year earlier had broken three world records and tied a fourth in a span of seventy minutes, wins gold medals in the 100-meter dash, 200-meter dash, 400-meter relay, and the long jump at the Munich Olympics, August 1936.

First Three-Time Indy Winner
race car driver Lou Meyer and his mechanic Lawson Harris win the 1936 Indy 500 and become the first triple winners.

Lou Gehrig,
a career .340 hitter, benches himself for a game at Detroit on May 2, 1939, "for the good of the team" after playing in 2,130 consecutive games.

1935, 1936, 1937, 1938, 1939

Ernie Lombardi
The slow-footed catcher wins the batting title, the MVP award, and catches Johnny Vander Meer's two consecutive no-hitters, 1938.

Babe Ruth
hits the final three homers of his career at Forbes Field in Pittsburgh, May 25, 1935. He retired June 2.

Sonja Henie
wins the gold medal in the 1936 Olympics, the third straight Olympics in which she won the gold for figure skating.

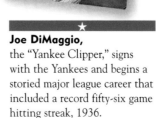

Joe DiMaggio,
the "Yankee Clipper," signs with the Yankees and begins a storied major league career that included a record fifty-six game hitting streak, 1936.

Wilbur Shaw
wins the Indianapolis three times between 1933 and 1940. After the war, he saved the track, and the Indianapolis 500, from oblivion.

HOW TO
Play 1st Base
ALL ★ SERIES 15¢
Hank GREENBERG
•
Jimmy FOXX

★
Hank Greenberg
is the first major league baseball player to volunteer for the service after the attack on Pearl Harbor, December 10, 1941.

CHAMP SIZE THIS MUCH MORE!
WHEATIES
"Breakfast of Champions"
RUTH-A-BAKED

1940, 1941, 1942, 1943, 1944

★
Ted Williams,
who batted .406 in 1941, enlists in the service in 1942, where, as a pilot, he experiments with boxing to stay in shape.

★
Stan Musial,
who played twenty-three seasons and compiled a .331 lifetime batting average with 3,630 hits and 475 home runs, breaks into the major leagues, 1941.

Joe Louis,
the heavyweight boxing champion, enlists as a private in the Army and goes on to serve four years before resuming his career in the ring, 1942.

START NOW TO PLAY
BETTER SOFTBALL
Get this new book by Ty Gleason and Arnie Simso
START WITH ANY TWO BOOKS!
Special Offer ORDER
FUTURE CHAMPIONS OF AMERICA SPORTS LIBRARY
✕ **WHEATIES** ✕

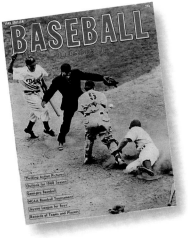

Patty Berg,
won the inaugural U.S. Women's Open in 1946.

Bob Mathias,
at the age of seventeen, becomes the youngest gold medalist in Olympic history, winning the decathlon, August 6, 1948.

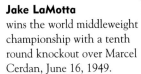

1945, 1946, 1947, 1948, 1949

Jake LaMotta
wins the world middleweight championship with a tenth round knockout over Marcel Cerdan, June 16, 1949.

Don Hutson
scores twenty-nine points in a single quarter of an NFL game on four touchdowns and five extra points, October 7, 1945.

Jack Armstrong explorer's sun watch

Citation,
with Eddie Arcaro riding, wins the Triple Crown of racing in 1948. The three-year-old thoroughbred won nineteen of twenty races that year.

Rocky Marciano
knocks out Jersey Joe Walcott in the thirteenth round to win the heavyweight championship, September 23, 1952.

The U.S.S.R.
participates in the Olympics for first time ever, in Helsinki, Finland. The Russians finish a close second to the United States in overall medals, 76-71, 1952.

Maureen Connolly
becomes the first woman to win the Grand Slam of tennis, at the age of eighteen, 1953. She would retire one year later due to injuries sustained in a fall from a horse.

1950, 1951, 1952, 1953, 1954

Bill Mosienko
of the Chicago Blackhawks scores three goals in twenty-one seconds against the Rangers at Madison Square Garden, March 23, 1952.

★

New York Yankees
become the only team to win five straight World Series, October 5, 1953.

Roger Bannister
runs the first four-minute mile in Oxford, England, with a time of 3:59.4 on May 6, 1954.

Ben Hogan
wins the British Open, July 10, 1953, becoming the first golfer to win the Masters, the U.S. Open, and the British Open in the same year.

Otto Graham
retires after leading the Cleveland Browns to ten straight championship games, winning seven, 1955.

1955, 1956, 1957, 1958, 1959

Jacques Plante,
the goalie who led the Montreal Canadiens to five straight Stanley Cup championships, becomes the first hockey player to wear a protective mask, 1959.

Wilt Chamberlain
enters the NBA after a stellar college career at Kansas and one year with the Harlem Globetrotters, 1959.

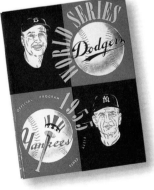

Gordie Howe

moves into first place on the all-time NHL scoring list, November 10, 1963.

Bob Gibson

throws his third complete game of the World Series for the Cardinals. St. Louis beats the Yankees in seven games, October 15, 1964.

1960, 1961, 1962, 1963, 1964

Roger Maris

hits his sixty-first home run of the season, breaking Babe Ruth's single-season record of sixty, October 1, 1961.

★

Wilt Chamberlain

scores 100 points for the Philadelphia Warriors in a game against the New York Knicks, March 2, 1962.

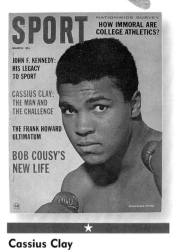

★

Cassius Clay

wins the heavyweight championship over heavily favored Sonny Liston, February 25, 1964. Fifteen months later, as Muhammad Ali, he defeats Liston again.

Jim Brown
announces his retirement while making a movie during the off-season. In nine seasons he became the NFL's all-time leading rusher with over 12,000 yards gained, 1966.

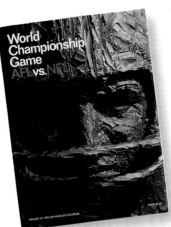

Super Bowl I
is played at the L.A. Coliseum with the NFL champion Green Bay Packers defeating the AFL champion Kansas City Chiefs 35-10, January 15, 1967.

1965, 1966, 1967, 1968, 1969

Pancho Gonzales
wins the longest tennis match ever played to date at Wimbledon in a five-set match that totaled 112 games, June 25, 1969.

Peggy Fleming
wins the gold medal in figure skating at the Winter Olympics in France, February 13, 1968.

Miracle Mets
win the World Series, defeating the Orioles four games to one to cap one of the greatest comebacks in baseball history, October 16, 1969. The Mets were in last place before the all-star break.

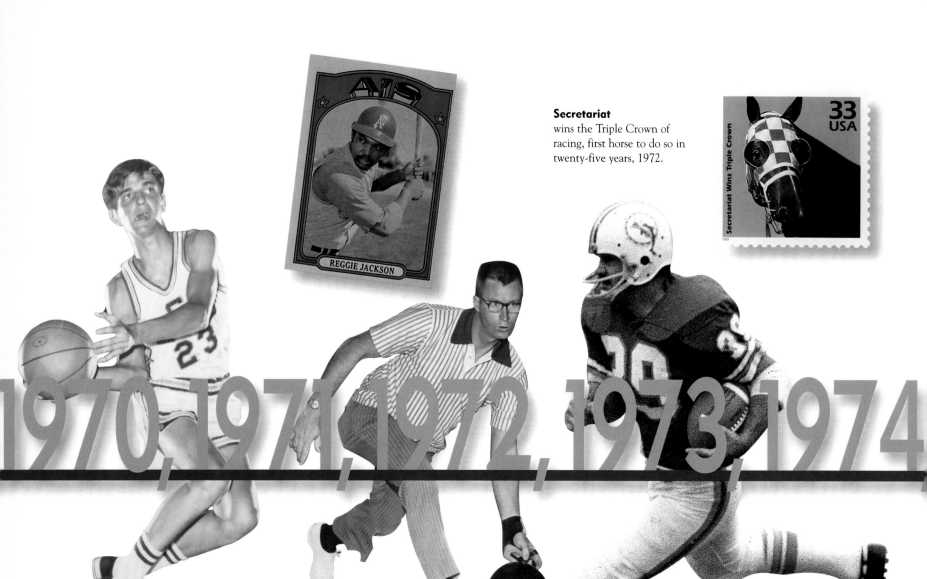

Secretariat
wins the Triple Crown of racing, first horse to do so in twenty-five years, 1972.

"Pistol Pete" Maravich
of LSU concludes his NCAA career with a record career scoring average of 44.2 points per game, March 1970.

Earl Anthony
wins the first of his record forty-one tournaments and leads the pro bowlers tour in scoring for the first time, 1973.

Miami Dolphins
finish 17-0 by defeating Washington 14-7 in Super Bowl VII. This is the only time in NFL history a team has finished undefeated, January 14, 1973.

Hank Aaron
breaks Babe Ruth's career home run record when he hits home run number 715 on April 8, 1974.

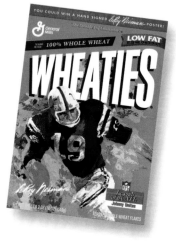

Tony Dorsett
wins the Heisman Trophy as the top college football player. His career rushing total shatters the former NCAA record by over 900 yards, 1976.

Billie Jean King
is named Female Athlete of the Year and defeats Bobby Riggs in the "Battle of the Sexes" match, September 20, 1973.

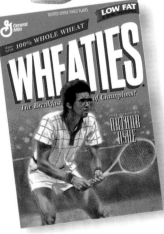

Johnny Bench
and the Cincinnati Reds' "Big Red Machine" win their second straight World Series by sweeping the Yankees, October 21, 1976.

Nancy Lopez
wins five consecutive tournaments and nine for the year as she wins her first LPGA championship, 1978.

Gerry Cheevers,
the Hall of Famer who painted stitches on his mask each time he was hit there by a puck, plays his seventeenth and final season, 1980.

Isiah Thomas
is named Final Four MVP as he leads Indiana to the NCAA championship, March 31, 1981.

John McEnroe,
a year after losing in what is called the greatest Wimbledon match ever to Björn Borg, defeats Borg at Wimbledon to win the championship, July 4, 1981.

1980, 1981, 1982, 1983, 1984,

Eric Heiden
sweeps all five speed skating gold medals for the U.S. at the Lake Placid Olympics, February 23, 1980.

Michael Jordan,
North Carolina freshman, sinks a game-winning jump shot in the final seconds to win the NCAA title, March 29, 1982.

Magic Johnson
leads the Lakers past the 76ers in six games to capture the NBA title in his rookie season, May 16, 1980.

Richard Petty
wins the Daytona 500 NASCAR race for the seventh and final time, February 15, 1981.

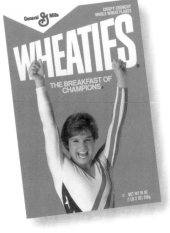

OFFICIAL GAME PROGRAM $5.00

SUPER BOWL XXI

DENVER BRONCOS VS. NEW YORK GIANTS

For the NFL Championship and the Vince Lombardi Trophy · Sunday, January 25, 1987 · Pasadena · 4:00 PM

Wayne Gretzky

After nine seasons in Edmonton where he captured eight MVPs, seven scoring titles, and four Stanley Cup championships, "The Great One" moves to L.A., August 9, 1988.

★

Joe Montana

leads the Forty-Niners 92 yards in eleven plays in the final minutes of Super Bowl XXIII to beat Cincinnati 20-16, January 22, 1989.

1985, 1986, 1987, 1988, 1989

Dwight Gooden,

National League Rookie of the Year the year in 1984, wins the Cy Young Award with a 24-4 record and 1.53 ERA, October 1985.

★

California Earthquake

on October 17, 1989, disrupts the Bay Area World Series between the Giants and the A's as the 7.1 temblor brings mass destruction. After a ten-day postponement the series resumed and Oakland finished their sweep.

★

Walter Payton

sets an NFL record with his eighth straight 100-yard rushing game but Bears lose their only game of the season to Miami, December 2, 1985.

1990, 1991, 1992, 1993, 1994,

WORLD SERIES
OFFICIAL
1991
FALL CLASSIC
SOUVENIR SCOREBOOK

★

Nolan Ryan
becomes the oldest pitcher to
throw a no-hitter with his
record seventh and final gem of
a twenty-seven year career,
striking out sixteen Toronto
Blue Jays, May 1, 1991.

★

Mario Lemieux
leads the Pittsburgh Penguins
to their first Stanley Cup,
beating the Minnesota North
Stars, May 25, 1991.

Monica Seles
becomes the youngest winner of
a Grand Slam tennis tournament
in the twentieth century when
she wins the French Open at
sixteen years old, June 6, 1990.

★

Michael Jordan
and teammate Scottie Pippen
lead the Chicago Bulls to their
first of six NBA championships
during the decade, 1991.

Bonnie Blair
wins two gold medals in speed
skating at the Winter Olympics
in Albertville, France, February
1992.

Steve Young

throws six touchdown passes and leads San Francisco to their fifth Super Bowl championship as the Forty-Niners bowl over the San Diego Chargers 49-26 in Miami, January 29, 1995.

Tara Lipinski,

at fourteen years old, becomes the youngest figure skater to win the world championship, March 22, 1997.

Pete Sampras

wins his twelfth Grand Slam title of the decade and sixth Wimbledon, tying Australia's Roy Emerson for most career Grand Slam titles, June 1999.

1995, 1996, 1997, 1998, 1999

U.S. Women's Ice Hockey Team

defeats Canada 3-1 to win the first gold medal awarded for women's hockey at the Olympics in Nagano, Japan, February 17, 1998.

2000, 2001, 2002

Since that time our role models have routinely made their way into our homes on radio and television, and into our kitchens printed on Wheaties boxes, where their triumphs can be relived by youngsters at the breakfast table. As the decades passed, athletes honored by having their successes celebrated on a Wheaties box came to represent a kind of hall of fame honoring certain inner qualities. Just as those feats have taken their places in our hearts and memories, the attributes of success have come to be recognized as the real value of athletic competition. The determination, courage, and perseverance so necessary to winning is balanced by the willingness of the great ones to sacrifice individual goals for the sake of the team. And all of it is overlaid by the grace emerging from such physical and spiritual exercise. ★

★

Tiger Woods
wins his third Masters Tournament and the seventh major of his career by shooting 12 under par at Augusta, April 14, 2002.

★

Sarah Hughes
wins gold medal in figure skating in Winter Olympics in Salt Lake City, Utah, February 2002.